To Mama from her loving
daughter.

I love you,

Rita

1-21-66

Poem Portraits
for All Occasions

by
JAMES J. METCALFE

Garden City, New York
HANOVER HOUSE

BOOKS BY JAMES J. METCALFE

Poem Portraits for All Occasions
Poem Portraits of Inspiration
Garden in My Heart
Poem Portraits
More Poem Portraits
Poem Portraits of the Saints
My Rosary of Rhymes
Love Portraits
Daily Poem Portraits
Poems for Children

All selections in this book are reprinted
by permission of Field Enterprises, Inc.

FOREWORD

Millions knew James J. Metcalfe as the author of the nationally syndicated column "Portraits." For twenty-two years people from coast to coast delighted in the simple verse that flowed from his pen. Many called him a poet. He called himself a writer of verse. But the distinction is academic, for the important thing was the beautiful words and thoughts which he produced. His verse stirred readers in newspapers throughout the United States, Canada, Mexico, and Ireland.

Jim Metcalfe was a lawyer, G-Man, and newspaper reporter before he began writing "Portraits" in 1938. He attended the University of Notre Dame and Loyola University in Chicago, where he received his law degree. During the early thirties he was a special agent in the FBI, and helped to bring to justice such notorious criminals as John Dillinger and Baby Face Nelson. After leaving the FBI, he became a newspaper reporter, and in 1935 won the National Headliners Club silver plaque for his undercover work in exposing the German and German-American Bunds.

I knew Jim Metcalfe, but of course I never called him Jim. To me, my sister Kris, and my brother Jimmie he was Daddy. To us he was a wonderful father, and to my mother he was a wonderful husband. We loved and respected Daddy. And should I write a foreword of a thousand pages, I could never so appropriately pay tribute to my father as well as did the Houston *Post* shortly after his death, in an editorial, the last line of which read:

"The world could do with more James J. Metcalfes."

DON METCALFE

CONTENTS BY SUBJECT

v

LOVE

OCCASION

OCCUPATION

PATRIOTISM

ix

PRAYER

xi

FORGET THE TRIVIAL

Why do we stop to bother with . . . The trivial things of life . . .
Like cutting melted butter with . . . A keen-edged carving knife?
. . . So many real important things . . . Are waiting to be done . . .
For any measure of success . . . In battles to be won . . . Why pick
up every paper clip . . . Or hairpin on the floor . . . When every-
where our brains and brawn . . . Are needed so much more? . . .
The same as conversation that . . . Is idle as can be . . . When we
could interchange good thoughts . . . And say them sensibly . . .
Let us forget the trivial things . . . And try to concentrate . . . On
those important matters we . . . Should not allow to wait.

AS GOD MAY CREDIT

God is our greatest creditor . . . While we are here on earth . . . And
many times He credits us . . . With more than we are worth . . . He
carries us along in life . . . Despite our mounting debts . . . And
when we say we're sorry, He . . . Forgives and He forgets . . . He
washes off our messy slates . . . And lets us start anew . . . And he
accepts the promises . . . That we propose to do . . . And even when
we fail again . . . He takes a kindly glance . . . And he decides to
give us all . . . Another fighting chance . . . So let us serve and love
Him and . . . Believe without a doubt . . . And pray that He will
never let . . . Our credit line run out.

HER MOVING MOODS

Today I moved the furniture . . . But that is nothing new . . . It has
become the common task . . . That I am told to do . . . My wife is
never satisfied . . . To leave things as they are . . . She always has a
plan she thinks . . . Is dandier by far . . . And if I try to argue, I . . .
Am only losing ground . . . As couch, piano, tables and . . . The
chairs get pushed around . . . She may be very clever in . . . Her
decorating schemes . . . But they disturb my leisure, and . . . They
haunt me in my dreams . . . I wish I had the nerve sometime . . .
When she is out of town . . . To place the furniture myself . . . And
nail the pieces down.

1

STILL IN MY HEART

I still have all the letters and . . . The little notes you sent . . . And every gift, however small . . . That was sincerely meant . . . Although they are but memories . . . How sweet those memories are! . . . Each one is like a rainbow or . . . A brilliant, silver star . . . Each is a magic guardian . . . That takes me by the hand . . . And guides me through the looking glass . . . Into a wonderland . . . A wonderland of all the past . . . So happily we shared . . . When I told you, and you told me . . . How lovingly we cared . . . The years have drifted into mist . . . Like ships that fade at sea . . . But I still hold your heart, my love . . . In every memory.

FOOD FOR THOUGHT

A meal is more than breakfast or . . . A dinner or a lunch . . . And more than what is casually . . . Referred to as a brunch . . . And it is more than liquids and . . . The solid foods we eat . . . From ham and eggs and coffee to . . . The grandest banquet treat . . . It is a necessary pause . . . A time to get together . . . To eat with those around us, and . . . To talk about the weather . . . A meal should not be started or . . . Digested all alone . . . There should be conversation to . . . Divide the smallest bone . . . Because whatever kind it is . . . Wherever cooked or bought . . . A meal should feed the body, and . . . Provide some food for thought.

FRIEND OF LONG AGO

It is so good to meet a friend . . . From many years ago . . . And talk about old times and all . . . The joys you used to know . . . Experiences wonderful . . . And some that made you scared . . . The many feelings mutual . . . The problems that you shared . . . And you may talk of certain friends . . . Whom now you see no more . . . As God decided for the best . . . In time of peace or war . . . It is so good to meet that friend . . . To see his smile again . . . And to discover he is much . . . The same as he was then . . . A pleasant and inspiring . . . Event in every way . . . It is as though you really found . . . The road to yesterday.

NEVER HOPELESS

As life goes on from day to day . . . And God is always near . . .
There is no place for hopelessness . . . There is no need to fear . . .
Lift up your eyes, behold the skies . . . The bright, the dark, the dim
. . . Whatever weather there may be . . . It is ordained by Him . . .
Do not despair because of some . . . Injustice done to you . . . Doubt
not all other souls on earth . . . Because of one or two . . . Do not
condemn yourself too much . . . For wrongs that you have done . . .
It may deplete your moral strength . . . In battles to be won . . .
Lift up your heart, have faith in God . . . And say a fervent prayer
. . . For as you trust in Him, so He . . . Will keep you in His care.

CHRISTMAS EVE

Tonight is holy Christmas Eve . . . Becoming Christmas Morn . . .
The night in Christian history . . . When Jesus Christ was born . . .
That joyous night in Bethlehem . . . When shepherds knelt in prayer
. . . While Mary kept her baby warm . . . With sweet and tender
care . . . The Son of God, our Saviour . . . Who lived and preached
and died . . . And to redeem our countless sins . . . Was scourged
and crucified . . . It is that holy time of year . . . When we should
kneel and pray . . . And thank Him for His birthday that . . . Is now
our Christmas Day . . . It is the time for all the world . . . To realize
that the past . . . The present and the future—all . . . Belong to God
at last.

HOME POLITICS

Politics are not confined . . . To government alone . . . Indeed,
right in our house we have . . . A brand that is our own . . . I do a
favor for my wife . . . And she does one for me . . . Though sometimes she or I must use . . . Real ingenuity . . . And then there are
the children who . . . Assume important roles . . . When all the
votes are recognized . . . In certain family polls . . . We make some
secret bargains but . . . Our politics are clean . . . We sling no mud,
and nobody . . . Is ever mad or mean . . . We have the party system
but . . . The party is all one . . . And that is why we always win
. . . And get our projects done.

STILL LOVE YOU

As long as I remember, love . . . My heart has been your own . . .
And to this very day I still . . . Belong to you alone . . . How could I
care for someone else . . . In all the wide world blue . . . When there
is really nobody . . . To quite compare with you? . . . Nobody else
could have your charm . . . Or your inviting smile . . . And no one
else could do so much . . . To make this life worth while . . . I loved
you many years ago . . . And in the time between . . . The vision of
your countless charms . . . Has never left the scene . . . Oh, let me
take you in my arms . . . And hold you close to me . . . And blend
today and every day . . . With our sweet memory.

GOD IS REAL

Faith in God is not a thing . . . That you are forced to take . . . You
are free to choose your course . . . Asleep or wide awake . . . No
civil government demands . . . That you acknowledge God . . . As
you pursue the daily path . . . That you decide to plod . . . But how
can you explain the fact . . . That you are here on earth . . . And
who is there to credit you . . . For what you may be worth? . . . You
know someday you have to die . . . As everybody must . . . And
when that moment comes to pass . . . You will return to dust . . .
And so it is quite obvious . . . There is a God above . . . As He allowed you to be born . . . And gives you all His love.

WE HOPE AND PRAY

Independence Day means more . . . Than our own liberty . . . It
should remind our hearts to help . . . The whole world to be free . . .
As much as we are capable . . . To make that dream come true . . .
For those who wish they had their choice . . . Of what to think and
do . . . Of course we cannot use our might . . . To loose their prison
door . . . Unless their captors force a fight . . . And we must go to
war . . . We do not want armed conflict now . . . By land and air
and sea . . . May God have mercy on us and . . . Prevent such tragedy . . . But we can teach democracy . . . And we can always pray
. . . That all the world someday will live . . . According to God's
way.

MY MIND WAKES UP

If I have some important thought . . . Or special date to keep . . . I say it to myself again . . . Before I go to sleep . . . I do not have to write it on . . . A pad of any kind . . . For it has been recorded in . . . A corner of my mind . . . And when the dawn arrives, and when . . . I wake up casually . . . The message that I took to bed . . . Returns at once to me . . . The same as when I go to bed . . . And set my clock to ring . . . I usually wake up before . . . I must turn off that thing . . . The answer is the human mind . . . Which can be trained to keep . . . Important dates and special notes . . . Through all the time we sleep.

SPECTATOR FUN

It's fun to follow sports upon . . . The television screen . . . But so much more if you can be . . . A fan right on the scene . . . You may not see some plays as well . . . As TV cameras show . . . Or understand as clearly as . . . Explained on radio . . . But there you are with all the crowd . . . So colorful and gay . . . To cheer your favorite team and help . . . Your heroes on their way . . . No living room can take the place . . . Of tickets by the pair . . . Or match the feeling wonderful . . . That you are really there . . . And where is any hot dog that . . . Is such a special treat . . . As that which stadium vendors would . . . Deliver to your seat?

HOMEWORK GOES ON

I thought my darling daughter, Kris . . . Was so advanced in school . . . I could not help with homework now . . . By thumb or any rule . . . Especially in learning French . . . Which is so strange to me . . . But she declares I only need . . . To test her memory . . . "Just read the English, Daddy dear . . . And I will spell and say . . . The phrases, sentences and words . . . Assigned to me today" . . . And so I still spend hours on . . . That high school coaching bench . . . Despite the simple truth that I . . . Am ignorant of French . . . Of course I love to help her and . . . I wish I could do more . . . But I do hope Français and I . . . Will soon say "au revoir."

MY THANKS TO YOU

If I have any thought of you . . . Or any memory . . . It is that you have always been . . . So wonderful to me . . . You have been sweet as sugar and . . . So true in every way . . . That there are not sufficient thanks . . . That I could ever say . . . I love you and I promise you . . . That we will never part . . . As long as you believe in me . . . And take me to your heart . . . I could not see another face . . . Or hold another hand . . . Or find a soul so willing now . . . To love and understand . . . And so whatever I may be . . . And all I ever do . . . If there is any credit, dear . . . It all belongs to you.

FRIEND FOREVER

Thank you for your friendly heart . . . For being kind and true . . . Thank you for each cheerful word . . . And just for being you . . . Friendship never meant so much . . . Until the day we met . . . Your every favor is the kind . . . I never could forget . . . Not just in time of tragedy . . . That causes wounds and scars . . . But also your rejoicing when . . . I gather lucky stars . . . I know I can rely on you . . . And lean upon your breast . . . And in your loyalty I feel . . . That I am richly blest . . . I thank you, and I promise you . . . Each moment, night and day . . . I am your friend for evermore . . . In every faithful way.

HOME SUNDAY DINNER

The Sunday family dinner should . . . Be always quite the best . . . And with all members present, it . . . Should be the happiest . . . And "Sunday" dinner also means . . . Those special times each year . . . Thanksgiving Day and Christmas and . . . A birthday very dear . . . With mom and dad and youngsters all . . . Around the festive table . . . To ask God's grace, then talk and eat . . . As much as they are able . . . It is that special day each week . . . When they can all be there . . . No one is overtime at work . . . In school or anywhere . . . The family united could . . . Not ask for any more . . . Except when one is absent who . . . Is being trained for war.

6

MOST IMPORTANT MAN

The most important man alive . . . In all our land today . . . Is he
who works from dawn to dusk . . . To get his weekly pay . . . The
little man who rides the bus . . . To factory or store . . . Or to some
office he has seen . . . A thousand times before . . . For as he fills his
job, and strives . . . To raise a family . . . He is the most essential
part . . . Of our economy . . . Without him we could never have . . .
The services and goods . . . That are the lifelines of our land . . .
And all our neighborhoods . . . And as he is the hero in . . . Our
daily fight to win . . . So his good wife is naturally . . . The lovely
heroine.

GOD, JUST FOR YOU

Help me, O God, to put away . . . My thinking and my schemes . . .
As much as I know full and well . . . That they are only dreams . . .
As much as I am conscious of . . . My poor ability . . . And each
ambition I pursue . . . Becomes futility . . . And yet I want to serve
You, God . . . In every way I can . . . Especially to bring some joy
. . . To every fellow man . . . I know I am not capable . . . To play
a perfect part . . . But everything I do for You . . . I do with all my
heart . . . So, help me, God, to do my best . . . And give me added
strength . . . That my poor efforts on this earth . . . May reach a
greater length.

WHO DIED FOR US

We march today in sadness, and . . . We march in sober joy . . . To
honor all our soldier dead . . . Each valiant man and boy . . . This is
our tribute to their life . . . And their untimely death . . . The heroes
of our country, to . . . The final, gasping breath . . . Yes, every one
of them deserves . . . The laurels of a hero . . . Whatever fear or
courage when . . . The hour stood at zero . . . No matter what his
final thought . . . Or his departing prayer . . . He will be honored
always, as . . . He more than did his share . . . With praise and gratitude we march . . . For all our soldier dead . . . Whose bravery has
filled the graves . . . Where we would be instead.

NEVER AWAY

Whenever I must leave you, dear . . . Wherever I may go . . . You
are forever in my heart . . . And every dream I know . . . You are as
much beside me as . . . The winds that touch my cheek . . . And in
each sound around me, dear . . . I seem to hear you speak . . . Oh, it
is not like seeing you . . . And holding you to me . . . Nothing could
ever take the place . . . Of your reality . . . No other sound could be
your voice . . . No other touch your hand . . . As only you must
know, my dear . . . And truly understand . . . But loving you as
deeply and . . . Completely as I do . . . However far away, I still . . .
Am not away from you.

GLOBE

A globe is truly practical . . . For office and for home . . . With all
the countries of the world . . . Where we might like to roam . . . It
shows the rivers and the seas . . . And how to find our way . . . From
Texas to Alaska and . . . New York to Mandalay . . . It marks the
borders of each land . . . That we are looking at . . . And helps us
realize that the earth . . . Is not exactly flat . . . The children like to
use it as . . . They learn geography . . . And it can settle arguments
. . . With true finality . . . A globe affords a chance to dream . . . Of
treasure-laden ships . . . And one way we can have the world . . .
Right at our fingertips.

BLESS YOU BOTH

A happy birthday, Jimmie dear . . . May all good things in life . . .
Be yours today and evermore . . . For you and your dear wife . . .
May you and darling Beverly . . . In love forever stay . . . And all
your dreams and hopes come true . . . In every perfect way . . .
Your mother and your brother and . . . Your sister sweet and I . . .
Are proud of your good progress through . . . The years that have
gone by . . . And for the years that lie ahead . . . We hope that God
will bless . . . Your life and Beverly's with all . . . Success and hap-
piness . . . A happy birthday, Jimmie, just . . . As happy as can be
. . . With love to you and your dear wife . . . From all your family.

MENTAL MOMENT OFF

There seldom is a time of day . . . That I may call my own . . . But
there are certain moments that . . . Belong to me alone . . . As now
and then I contemplate . . . The world before my eyes . . . And steal
a second silently . . . To gaze up at the skies . . . Those are the instant breathing spells . . . I take to contemplate . . . Why people act
the way they do . . . What makes them love or hate . . . And also to
appraise myself . . . The faults that I possess . . . And what I ought
to do to gain . . . Some honorable success . . . It only takes a second
small . . . Including time to say . . . The SOS I send to God . . .
To help me on my way.

SO LONG TO SCHOOL

Vacation time is here again . . . Farewell to books and chalk . . .
And all the problems and the rules . . . Of which the teachers talk
. . . The boys and girls are happy as . . . They hurry out the door
. . . With many weeks ahead in which . . . The bell will ring no
more . . . It is the time for swimming and . . . For picnics under
trees . . . For travel to the mountains or . . . A breath of ocean
breeze . . . Forgotten is the homework that . . . Was sometimes hard
to do . . . And vanished is the longing now . . . To study something
new . . . Except the way to sail a boat . . . Or how to ride a horse
. . . Or pass examination in . . . Some other pleasure course.

BEST HOLIDAYS

Holidays are wonderful . . . With all the best of cheer . . . And more
especially when they . . . Surround a family dear . . . When loved
ones come from near and far . . . To celebrate together . . . And all
is love and harmony . . . Regardless of the weather . . . Holidays
composed of smiles . . . Each one a soft caress . . . And little tears
that fill the heart . . . Those tears of happiness . . . At Easter or
Thanksgiving or . . . The Christmastime vacation . . . Some birthday, anniversary . . . Or other celebration . . . All holidays are wonderful . . . Whatever time or place . . . But best of all are those
when all . . . The family may embrace.

AS YOU ARE GLAD

I cannot prove I love you, dear . . . You have to take my word . . .
Despite whatever whisperings . . . And gossip you have heard . . .
Despite my failure to appear . . . When you expected me . . . And
all the promises I made . . . That now are memory . . . Perhaps
I failed you once or twice . . . Or maybe even more . . . But my
sincerest rings and knocks . . . Have been right at your door . . . I
cannot prove I love you, and . . . Your heart may not believe . . .
Whenever you are gone, it is . . . The only time I grieve . . . But you
mean all the world to me . . . And I am never sad . . . As long as I
have reason to . . . Believe that you are glad.

BELIEVE AND PRAY

In trial and adversity . . . Let not your faith grow dim . . . But say a
fervent prayer to God . . . And keep your trust in Him . . . Let hope
not wither on the vine . . . Of sorrow and despair . . . Remember
God knows everything . . . And He is everywhere . . . However
dark the day may seem . . . Or frightening the night . . . All troubles
fade and disappear . . . And life turns out all right . . . Provided you
maintain your faith . . . And do not yield to fear . . . The while you
pray for courage with . . . A heart that is sincere . . . Resign yourself most humbly now . . . To do God's holy will . . . And He will
surely bless you and . . . Your least request fulfill.

WE NEED NO MAT

When I go calling on a friend . . . It's only natural that . . . I never
look around his stoop . . . To find a welcome mat . . . I know that I
am welcome as . . . I knock upon his door . . . However often I have
been . . . To visit him before . . . I know that he will ask me in . . .
To stay as long and late . . . As my appointments here and there . . .
And other things can wait . . . And when he comes to call on me . . .
He need not be demure . . . Nor search for signs of any kind
. . . To make him feel secure . . . He knows that at the instant
of . . . His friendly knock or ring . . . He will be just as welcome
as . . . The flowers are in spring.

RESENTMENT

Resentment is a bitterness . . . That eats the heart away . . . When we feel quite insulted by . . . What others do or say . . . It is a human frailty . . . Not easy to suppress . . . And yet it only helps destroy . . . Our peace and happiness . . . It prods the mind to seek revenge . . . For mental injury . . . When probably our fancied wound . . . Is just our jealousy . . . If now sincerely we believe . . . Injustice has been done . . . There always is a court of law . . . Where battles may be won . . . But plain resentment is no way . . . To settle any score . . . It only shuts out friendship as . . . It locks and bolts the door.

MARKET PLACE

The market place is wonderful . . . With products that are good . . . And prices that defy the stores . . . In any neighborhood . . . Of course you have to purchase them . . . In larger quantity . . . Yet certain items do provide . . . For real economy . . . Like bushels of tomatoes and . . . Of peaches and of pears . . . That you may want to cook and can . . . To store beneath the stairs . . . Fresh sea food is available . . . Fish, shrimp, and lobster tails . . . Oysters, clams, and quahogs caught . . . Beneath New England sails . . . The market place is wonderful . . . But as for staple goods . . . The stores that save you money are . . . Right in all neighborhoods.

TAKE SPECIAL CARE

Thanksgiving Day is almost here . . . Be careful how you drive . . . On highway and on city street . . . If you would stay alive . . . Do visit friends and relatives . . . For all good things to share . . . But, please, when you are traveling . . . Take care, take care, take care . . . Enjoy your turkey, dressing and . . . The whipped-cream pumpkin pie . . . And when the meal is over, just . . . Lean back, relax and sigh . . . Add up the blessings wonderful . . . That you enjoy today . . . As God has been so good to you . . . And yours in every way . . . Do have a nap to make you feel . . . Refreshed, alert, awake . . . So you can drive home safely for . . . Your loving family's sake.

NO MORE THAN BEFORE

If now I seem to love you more . . . Than when I first met you . . .
Believe me, dearest, when I say . . . It simply is not true . . . Because
when we were introduced . . . My eyes could clearly see . . . That
never anybody else . . . Could mean so much to me . . . Yes, all my
love became your own . . . Forever and a day . . . Unselfishly, sincerely and . . . In every other way . . . And it has always been like
that . . . Throughout the months and years . . . As we have shared
our deepest thoughts . . . Our hopes and smiles and tears . . . And
so as you are everything . . . That I am living for . . . How could it
now be possible . . . For me to love you more?

MY BOSS KNOWS BEST

I have the offer of a raise . . . Which ought to be enough . . . But as
my boss is weakening . . . I think I should get tough . . . I should
demand a whole lot more . . . As now his prospects dim . . . And as
he needs me, I appear . . . More valuable to him . . . And yet it
does not seem quite fair . . . To treat him in that way . . . His offer
may exceed the sum . . . He can afford to pay . . . And always in so
many ways . . . He has been good to me . . . Including his sincere
concern . . . About my family . . . I am not interested in wealth . . .
Or pampering my pride . . . And so I think I'll go along . . . With
what he may decide.

BLESS YOU, SISTER

Happy birthday, Sister, and . . . God's blessing be on you . . . For
all the many wonderful . . . And kindly things you do . . . To teach
the children in your class . . . Piano, violin . . . And harps that
sound angelic songs . . . To keep the world from sin . . . For every
word of wisdom and . . . Each night and morning prayer . . . That
you bestow on boys and girls . . . Entrusted to your care . . . God
bless your perseverance on . . . This birthday, Sister dear . . . As you
have served Him faithfully . . . Each day and month and year . . .
No happy birthday wish could be . . . More loving or more true . . .
Than this one that your brother sends . . . With pride and joy to
you.

LUCKY IS HE

The man most fortunate in life . . . Is he who finds his place . . .
Who does the task he wants to do . . . And knows what he must face
. . . The one whose search is ended and . . . Who does not have to
grope . . . Whose life no longer hinges on . . . The door of simple
hope . . . For he is happy in his work . . . And he will pass the test
. . . The same as each contented soul . . . Can always do its best . . .
Unfortunately in this life . . . He is just one of few . . . Who learn in
time what they were born . . . Most qualified to do . . . We are not
all so lucky now . . . But God will bless each man . . . Regardless of
his place on earth . . . Who does the best he can.

GOD AT OUR SIDE

God is forever at our side . . . Wherever we may be . . . In every
happy moment and . . . In time of tragedy . . . In every disappoint-
ment and . . . Each wonderful surprise . . . And all the lonely moments that . . . Are filled with tears and sighs . . . In every shadow
on the path . . . Where we may walk today . . . And to the farthest
corner of . . . The world where we may stray . . . God hears our every
whisper, and . . . He listens to each prayer . . . And so we have no
reason to . . . Be sad or to despair . . . God is forever at our side
. . . We have no need to fear . . . As much as we have faith in Him
. . . And we are real sincere.

U. S. CHAPLAIN

The chaplain is a serviceman . . . Who helps out everywhere . . . To
comfort soldiers, sailors, and . . . The ones who guard the air . . .
He is an officer, but that . . . Does not promote his pride . . . As he
is only interested . . . That God is on our side . . . That every serviceman believes . . . In time of peace or war . . . The principles of
liberty . . . We always struggle for . . . He may be priest or rabbi or
. . . A minister quite brave . . . Who counsels men in service or . . .
Who dedicates a grave . . . But every chaplain is a man . . . So wise
in many ways . . . Who helps our sons in uniform . . . And earns our
lasting praise.

AS YOU ARE WITH ME

Could you be patient, dearest one . . . And could you go along . . .
If all the world were upside down . . . And everything seemed
wrong? . . . Could you contain your temper if . . . You thought I
were to blame? . . . Or would you just ignore me and . . . Forget my
humble name? . . . How much would you believe in me . . . If nothing turned out right? . . . How long would you remain with me . . .
To wage a desperate fight? . . . The answer to each question, dear
. . . Is solely up to you . . . And my own love depends upon . . .
Whatever you would do . . . Unless your faith and promises . . .
Could last for evermore . . . It would be better, darling, now . . . If
we just closed the door.

A LA CARTE

I have encountered restaurants . . . With culinary art . . . And most
of them have taught me I . . . Should order a la carte . . . I mean
those special places where . . . Each dish is excellent . . . And every
bit of food is worth . . . The money that is spent . . . The dinners
are delicious and . . . Each one is quite a treat . . . But for a person
such as I . . . There is too much to eat . . . The cocktail, soup and
crackers and . . . The salad on the side . . . And then the entree
which is tall . . . And just as long and wide . . . I do enjoy those
dinners or . . . At least a certain part . . . But I would be much better off . . . To order a la carte.

YOU HELP ME SO

Your friendship means so much to me . . . In life from day to day
. . . You seem to be my guardian . . . In duty and in play . . . I
know that I may call on you . . . Whatever need may be . . . And
there is nothing I may ask . . . You will not do for me . . . In countless ways your friendship is . . . An inspiration true . . . However far
away I am . . . And out of touch with you . . . You give me courage,
faith and hope . . . In everything I try . . . And when I want a favor,
friend . . . You never ask me why . . . I thank you and I promise
you . . . Whenever you may call . . . Whatever you desire, I . . .
Will give my very all.

AS WE GET OLDER

Why do we think in terms of age . . . As human life goes on? . . . Why are we envious of youth . . . Of beauty and of brawn? . . . As God designed all life on earth . . . So youth must pass away . . . And there is never cause for shame . . . To tell our age today . . . While as for beauty and for brawn . . . There is no need to be . . . In rivalry with someone young . . . For either quality . . . There is a beauty of the soul . . . That only age can bring . . . And mental brawn in character . . . As strong as anything . . . Why work on body and on face . . . To try to hide the truth . . . When we have grown intelligent . . . Beyond the reach of youth.

SADNESS

Sadness is a feeling that . . . Is fancied or is true . . . Accordingly as people think . . . And what they like to do . . . Sadness is the sentiment . . . That draws a loving tear . . . When somebody has passed away . . . Who was so very dear . . . But sadness can be just as real . . . When someone says good-by . . . For just the shortness of a while . . . That brings a passing sigh . . . And sadness can be comforting . . . For those who want to weep . . . As they feel sorry for themselves . . . And lose a lot of sleep . . . Sadness is a feeling that . . . Is truly deep and sad . . . Or that emotion which may help . . . Some people to be glad.

HONEYMOON'S END

Young married people seem to think . . . A honeymoon should be . . . A paradise of happiness . . . For all eternity . . . Indeed it would be wonderful . . . If honeymoons could last . . . Until the world came to an end . . . And all of life was past . . . But it is not that simple, and . . . We have to face the truth . . . As marriage is forever, and . . . We cannot cling to youth . . . It calls for sacrifices and . . . Those hardships we must bear . . . With patience and with tolerance . . . And ever loving care . . . No honeymoon is permanent . . . Unless we can maintain . . . Our mutual love through family storms . . . Of wind and sleet and rain.

I WANT YOU ALWAYS

I want to be with you, my love . . . Wherever you may go . . . In happiness and sadness and . . . In sunshine, rain and snow . . . On city street and country lane . . . Beyond the seven seas . . . In all your dreams and evermore . . . In all your memories . . . I beg of you with all my heart . . . Please do not ever leave me . . . And please do not do anything . . . To hurt my heart and grieve me . . . I could not live without your love . . . Your kind, devoted heart . . . I could not bear the agony . . . Of being far apart . . . You are so wonderful, my love . . . You mean so much to me . . . I want to hold you in my arms . . . Now and eternally.

CIGARS SMELL RICH

My wife and daughter tell me that . . . Delightfully they itch . . . To have me smoke cigars because . . . Their odor is so rich . . . Or should I call it fragrance?—no . . . It sounds too flowery . . . For men who take a certain pride . . . In masculinity . . . But I admit there is an air . . . Of richness in cigars . . . With pleasing scents in office, home . . . And all the latest cars . . . I like to smoke them now and then . . . Especially when I . . . Am in a conference, because . . . It helps the time go by . . . You may not have much money and . . . No magic selling pitch . . . But one cigar can make you feel . . . And smell like you are rich.

VETERANS' DAY

God bless our noble veterans . . . The ones who fought and died . . . And everybody who put on . . . That uniform with pride . . . The dear departed and the ones . . . Who wear their wounds today . . . And those more fortunate who still . . . Engage in work and play . . . Each soldier and each sailor . . . And each guardian of the sky . . . Who fought for freedom when he knew . . . That he might have to die . . . We honor all of them, and we . . . Extend our humble thanks . . . For all the courage they displayed . . . Whatever were their ranks . . . And now we hope our veterans . . . Have made their final score . . . As we ask God to keep us safe . . . From any future war.

16

TO TAKE THE BLAME

When something has been done to which . . . There is attached some
shame . . . Do you become a hero if . . . You try to take the blame?
. . . I think it all depends upon . . . The special circumstance . . .
And what there is involved when you . . . Decide to take that
chance . . . If only you will suffer by . . . The punishment you take
. . . Then yours may be a noble deed . . . For someone else's sake
. . . But if somebody else is hurt . . . By what you want to do . . .
Then you are very wrong, and there . . . Is no excuse for you . . . Or
if your act should somehow help . . . To cover up a crime . . . Your
guilt is just as equal and . . . You should be "doing time."

THIS NEW YEAR, GOD

Give us, O God, the grace we need . . . To live this new year right
. . . With faith and hope and trust in You . . . Each morning, noon
and night . . . Inspire us to nobler heights . . . Of love and charity
. . . Unto our smallest neighbor and . . . Our tallest enemy . . .
Endow us with the wisdom and . . . The courage that we need . . .
To serve You loyally, O God . . . In thought and word and deed
. . . Without your help there is no help . . . That we can ever give
. . . Without Your gift of air to breathe . . . We could not even
live . . . And when temptation trips us and . . . We stumble on our
way . . . Forgive us, God, and help us up . . . To start a better day.

DEAR VALENTINE

When I was just a growing child . . . It was quite naturally . . . Each
Valentine that I received . . . Would much embarrass me . . . But
now the years have passed, and I . . . Have grown a little more . . .
And as it is St. Valentine's . . . I knock upon your door . . . I offer
you not just a card . . . A candy box or flowers . . . But all the seconds of my time . . . My minutes and my hours . . . I am in love
with you, my dear . . . I truthfully admit . . . And nothing ever in
my life . . . Can make a change in it . . . Please promise me that
you will be . . . My Valentine today . . . And hold me in your loving heart . . . In every happy way.

THE ONLY ONE

You are the only one for me . . . In all I think and do . . . And I just
feel somehow, my dear . . . That I belong to you . . . I want to take
you in my arms . . . And hold you close each day . . . And be your
humble servant, sweet . . . In every noble way . . . You are so generous to me . . . So wonderful and kind . . . Encouraging my hopeful
heart . . . Inspiring my mind . . . You make each sacrifice seem small
. . . The darkest sky look light . . . Yes, even through the fog or rain
. . . The stars appear at night . . . Believe me when I tell you, dear
. . . I am in love with you . . . And when I promise you that I . . .
Will be forever true.

READERS' VIEWS

Among the features that appear . . . In papers large and small . . .
The best one is the space reserved . . . For readers, one and all . . .
Where anybody in the world . . . From millionaire to minion
. . . Has equal chance in printer's ink . . . To give his own opinion
. . . He may agree or disagree . . . On issues of the day . . . Or he
may blast the paper in . . . A disrespectful way . . . But if the words
are fit to print . . . And there is space to use it . . . The fearless edi-
tor is one . . . Who never will refuse it . . . And so all readers have a
share . . . In freedom of the press . . . According to the different
views . . . That they would like to stress.

YOUR NEIGHBOR

Your neighbor is not only he . . . Who lives next door to you . . .
But also someone blocks away . . . Along your avenue . . . And also
everyone in town . . . And in the countryside . . . Throughout the
county and the state . . . And even nationwide . . . Your neighbor is
the strangest soul . . . Across the seven seas . . . As God would have
our hearts unite . . . In human sympathies . . . Your neighbor is your
fellowman . . . However far away . . . As all of us are brothers now
. . . In God's good world today . . . But only you, and you alone . . .
Can make that dream come true . . . By treating everyone as though
. . . He lived next door to you.

TREASURES

Treasures need not be composed . . . Of silver or of gold . . . They can be trinkets kept just for . . . The sentiment they hold . . . A picture or a lock of hair . . . A flower gently pressed . . . A ribbon or a kerchief that . . . Some gentle hand caressed . . . A ticket stub and program or . . . A shell from out the sea . . . Some very special letters or . . . A secret diary . . . Treasures can be all of these . . . And they can mean much more . . . Than all the handsome checks and gifts . . . Delivered at our door . . . Each is a treasured memory . . . A smile, a song, a sigh . . . A souvenir invaluable . . . Of months and years gone by.

DEAR DON AND LINDA

God bless you, Don and Linda, and . . . Your promise to be true . . . To one another all through life . . . In all you think and do . . . Bless your engagement vow, your love . . . The ring and every kiss . . . And may you be united soon . . . In wondrous wedding bliss . . . Dear son, I am so glad you chose . . . This girl so sweet and true . . . And I am so delighted, Don . . . That she accepted you . . . Dear Linda, you are charming and . . . So much in love with life . . . I know that you will be to Don . . . A sweet, devoted wife . . . And so my blessing to you both . . . And also let me say . . . It was so good that you became . . . Engaged on Mother's Day.

SCHOOL GOES ON

School is coming to an end . . . About this time of year . . . And many are the boys and girls . . . Who celebrate and cheer . . . But school is never over, in . . . Another way of speaking . . . As knowledge is a certain thing . . . That we are always seeking . . . Yes, even youngsters in their play . . . Throughout vacation days . . . Are learning how to swim and fish . . . And grow in other ways . . . Their education goes right on . . . Perhaps a bit more pleasant . . . Because they have more fun with those . . . Instructors who are present . . . But school is never over when . . . Dismissed is any class . . . For there are always tests in life . . . That each of us must pass.

A SMALL SURPRISE

I have a small surprise for you . . . If you will lend your ear . . . I
really am in love with you . . . And cherish you, my dear . . . You
wondered if I wanted you . . . You doubted day and night . . . And
maybe in your fondest dreams . . . You hoped that I would write
. . . But what is more important now . . . Is that you care for me
. . . And that I want to be your own . . . In every memory . . . I
could not call you, darling, and . . . I had no time to write . . .
But every evening in my heart . . . I told your heart good night . . .
And as you may have doubted me . . . And as you still are true . . .
You may be certain that I have . . . A small surprise for you.

AS YOU LOVE GOD

God loves you when your dreams are bright . . . And when your
hopes are dim . . . As long as you are humble and . . . You place
your faith in Him . . . He will protect and help your soul . . . Wherever you may be . . . In joy and glory of success . . . Or deepest
tragedy . . . God always watches over you . . . As He allowed your
birth . . . To carry on creation, and . . . To populate the Earth . . .
Sometimes your life may seem quite strange . . . And hard to understand . . . But always somewhere, in some way . . . There is His
guiding hand . . . And as you thank God humbly, and . . . You
try to be sincere . . . There will be nothing in this life . . . You
ever have to fear.

ON NEW YEAR'S EVE

There will be those who celebrate . . . Tonight as New Year's Eve
. . . That starts another year in which . . . To conquer and achieve
. . . While others will be occupied . . . With taking inventory . . .
And hoping that their book of life . . . Will show a balanced story
. . . There will be those who do not care . . . And those who strive
to add . . . Their sins against their kindly deeds . . . To make their
neighbors glad . . . Yes, some will have their fling tonight . . .
With worldly celebration . . . While others turn their thoughts to
God . . . In holy contemplation . . . In contemplation of their
strength . . . To face the daily strife . . . And by the grace of God
to start . . . Another year of life.

WHO WORK FOR PEACE

As there is hope for peace on earth . . . And there are those who strive . . . For better understanding and . . . To keep that hope alive . . . As there are those who struggle now . . . To do away with war . . . And try to spread democracy . . . To every foreign shore . . . I dedicate these lines to them . . . And say this special prayer . . . That God will always bless and guide . . . Their efforts everywhere . . . May infidels and tyrants see . . . The error of their ways . . . So all the brotherhood of man . . . May share in brighter days . . . I pray for courage in our time . . . That we may prove our worth . . . And by the grace of God achieve . . . True peace upon this earth.

FRIENDLY CALENDAR

The calendar upon my desk . . . Reminds me of a friend . . . And also that another year . . . Is very soon to end . . . His name has been before my eyes . . . Each day throughout the year . . . And many times the sight of it . . . Has brought me hope and cheer . . . I did not need the calendar . . . To keep him in my mind . . . But I am grateful that he was . . . So thoughtful and so kind . . . Because it was most helpful as . . . I looked at it each day . . . To check my working schedule and . . . My dates to rest and play . . . I wish I had a calendar . . . To send him for next year . . . Not to remind him of my name . . . But just my thanks sincere.

NO TIME TO RETIRE

Sometimes grandparents think that they . . . Can take a backward seat . . . As they have done their duty towards . . . The children at their feet . . . They think their children are secure . . . And they will take good care . . . Of every little baby that . . . Becomes another heir . . . But they are somewhat selfish when . . . They harbor that desire . . . Parental age is no excuse . . . For people to retire . . . Grandparents should not go their way . . . And leave the world to us . . . But in some measure, as they can . . . They should be generous . . . Their obligation to this life . . . Is not completely done . . . As long as they can be of help . . . In battles to be won.

MY WORLD, MY ALL

You are my life, my world, my all . . . In every happy way . . .
You are tomorrow in my heart . . . Today and yesterday . . . Your
love is all I ever want . . . The sunshine of your smile . . . Your
understanding nature and . . . Your goodness all the while . . . I
cherish you, my darling, as . . . I hold you in my arms . . . No
other one could be so sweet . . . Or ever match your charms . . .
However dark the sky may grow . . . Or wild the widest sea . . .
You will forever be the one . . . Whose heart belongs to me . . .
Wherever I may go, my love . . . Or what I strive to do . . . I
am your own forever, dear . . . My life belongs to you.

HAPPY MEETING

Nothing is more pleasant than . . . A happy meeting when . . . You
have not seen a friend for years . . . And now you meet again . . .
So often it is suddenly . . . When this occurs to you . . . But for
that very reason it . . . Is more delightful too . . . You try to fill
in all the time . . . You have not seen each other . . . As though
that long-lost person were . . . A sister or a brother . . . It is so
good to meet again . . . With some familiar face . . . And hurriedly
or gradually . . . Recall each time and place . . . And then to fill
the gap and bring . . . Your knowledge up to date . . . Your progress, family and how . . . You added so much weight.

BIRTHDAY SALUTE

We honor Washington today . . . And praise his stature high . . .
Who fought for liberation and . . . Was not afraid to die . . . He
had his faults and made mistakes . . . The same as all on earth . . .
But just as surely in his time . . . He proved his solid worth . . .
His motive was the noblest and . . . His heart was most sincere
. . . And nothing could dissuade him from . . . His will to persevere
. . . A general and statesman and . . . Our great first President . . .
He proved that every word he said . . . Was one he really meant . . .
Let us salute his birthday and . . . Pay homage to his name . . .
George Washington, who well deserves . . . His everlasting fame.

A BIKE WON'T DO

I used to ride a bicycle . . . When I was just a boy . . . It was a
handsome present and . . . It was my pride and joy . . . To school
and home, or to the store . . . Or just some place to play . . . It
took me everywhere I went . . . Without the least delay . . . And
then I got myself a job . . . And distance grew so far . . . There
was no choice, I simply had . . . To ride the trolley car . . . But
never did I reach the stage . . . Of autos old or new . . . They were
the prized possessions of . . . The very wealthy few . . . Whereas
today a car appears . . . To be no luxury . . . Most teen-age youngsters claim it is . . . A real necessity.

GOD KNOWS ALL

God always watches over us . . . Each moment, day and night . . .
As He beholds all things, so we . . . Are never out of sight . . .
He sees our every movement and . . . He hears each word we speak
. . . He knows what we are thinking and . . . Our feelings proud or
meek . . . He understands our frailty . . . As humans on this earth
. . . And how it sometimes weights the scales . . . Of our eternal
worth . . . Nothing escapes the mind of God . . . No smile or any
tear . . . No selfish thought or sinful act . . . Or any prayer sincere
. . . Yes, God is kind but also He . . . Is just in every way . . . Re-
warding good and punishing . . . The ones who disobey.

DEAR SON AND WIFE

God bless you, Don and Linda, dear . . . As you are man and wife
. . . And grant you all the happiness . . . And fruitfulness of life
. . . God bless you, son, and daughter new . . . Your life will surely
be . . . Forever joined in all your dreams . . . And every memory
. . . You love each other, and I know . . . That you will never
part . . . Because with gold and silver rings . . . Each of you
pledged your heart . . . May all your days for all your years . . . Be
filled with sunshine bright . . . And stars of joy and fortune good
. . . Surround your every night . . . And as unto each other you . . .
Will be forever true . . . May your dear babies be as sweet . . . And
wonderful as you.

SAFE WITH YOU

I cannot help but love you when . . . I think of all the days . . .
That we have been together in . . . So many happy ways . . . I
love you for your charming self . . . Your kindnesses to me . . .
But most of all I love you for . . . Dependability . . . No matter
what may happen, you . . . Are always at my side . . . To fill my
heart with solace and . . . With confidence and pride . . . I never
have to worry, for . . . I know that you are there . . . To comfort
me and kiss me and . . . To keep me in your care . . . And that is
why I love you, dear . . . With sentiment true . . . My hopes,
my dreams, and all of me . . . Are always safe with you.

PUBLIC LIBRARY

The public library to me . . . Is more than what it seems . . . It is
the peaceful haven of . . . A castle cloaked in dreams . . . Its
shelves are stairways to the stars . . . Its books are magic keys . . .
That turn the locks to treasure vaults . . . Of wistful reveries . . .
I journey to exotic lands . . . Beyond the oceans blue . . . And
every silent longing is . . . Another wish come true . . . I am the
singer of gay songs . . . The hero in a play . . . I am the prince
who kisses her . . . And carries her away . . . The air is filled with
music, and . . . My youthful heart is stout . . . Until the aisles
are empty, and . . . The lights are going out.

PROMOTION REAL

Promotion in a job or rank . . . Is real inspiring . . . So many are
the benefits . . . And joys that it can bring . . . A higher grade
and income and . . . More ease and luxury . . . For every member
of a good . . . And loving family . . . But no promotion is worth
while . . . That is not really earned . . . As, for example, when the
wheels . . . Of influence have turned . . . When someone speaks
the smallest word . . . Or makes the slightest sign . . . Instructing
that a certain name . . . Should jump ahead in line . . . Promotion
has no value if . . . It is not well deserved . . . Accordingly as he or
she . . . Most competently served.

NO HANDOUTS

Some people look for favors as . . . They go along their way . . .
Throughout their working hours or . . . When they relax and play
. . . Not just the little favors that . . . Are common courtesy . . .
But also those that go beyond . . . The call of charity . . . They
do not seem to understand . . . Or they have never learned . . .
That certain favors they request . . . Are those that should be
earned . . . They only think about themselves . . . And how much
they can get . . . And as for giving in return . . . They have not
started yet . . . But special favors are bestowed . . . On only those
who serve . . . In public or in private life . . . As much as they deserve.

TRAVEL AGENT

Your travel agent is indeed . . . The finest friend you know . . .
To solve your problems, large or small . . . Wherever you may go
. . . He can arrange your trip for you . . . Around the world and
back . . . And be your guardian angel for . . . The knowledge you
may lack . . . Your passport, vaccination, and . . . Accommodation
range . . . The cost of children, baggage, and . . . Of currency exchange . . . Which sights to see, what clothes to wear . . . According
to your purse . . . And how to get in contact with . . . A doctor or
a nurse . . . He is your guide to happiness . . . Your travel agent
true . . . Just call him up—in every way . . . He will take care of
you.

IDEAL HOUSEWIFE

There is a wife who cooks and works . . . Around the house all day
. . . And one whose interest mainly is . . . To run around and play
. . . There is the sweet, submissive wife . . . Who wants to serve
her man . . . And she who pampers just herself . . . As richly as she
can . . . And then there is the in-between . . . The one with balanced mind . . . Who does her duties but expects . . . Her husband
to be kind . . . To help around the house a bit . . . And do it with
a smile . . . And take her out to dine and dance . . . If just once
in a while . . . She is the ideal housewife and . . . If he has any
sense . . . He will reward her now and then . . . Regardless of expense.

NEVER TRITE

There are so many phrases that . . . Grow trite from year to year . . . But never that expression old . . . To say, "I love you, dear" . . . And as a thousand times my lips . . . Have said it to you then . . . I do not hesitate, my love . . . To say it once again . . . Those are the words that never age . . . And make nobody weary . . . But do so much to lift the heart . . . That is alone and dreary . . . "I love you"—it is like a song . . . That cannot ever die . . . Because it means, "I want you, dear . . . With never a good-by" . . . And so I keep on saying it . . . With every feeling true . . . As I am really certain, dear . . . I am in love with you.

GOD LOVES PRAYERS

As God so often helps you with . . . Your struggles and your cares . . . Be happy, and remember now . . . To say your daily prayers . . . Your morning prayer of gratitude . . . That you awoke once more . . . With time on earth to carry on . . . And to improve your score . . . And then your evening prayer of thanks . . . For one more night of rest . . . And every way throughout the day . . . You were so kindly blest . . . God loves all prayers, especially . . . The ones at dawn and night . . . And when you say them, you will find . . . Your future looking bright . . . And if you have some extra time . . . One moment small or two . . . Give thanks to God again because . . . He is so good to you.

HELP OTHERS SMILE

When friends feel sorry for themselves . . . And are inclined to pout . . . There is a simple little way . . . To sort of help them out . . . And that is to pretend that you . . . Are wholly unaware . . . That there is any bitterness . . . Or sadness in the air . . . Then suddenly, though casually . . . Say something really funny . . . If only silly words to make . . . The sky look somewhat sunny . . . The chances are that they will laugh . . . And right away forget . . . Whatever thing it was that caused . . . The mind to get upset . . . And just to see them glad again . . . Will make you happy too . . . For that small act of charity . . . You took the time to do.

NO WATCH OR CLOCK

I do not want a watch or clock . . . As any kind of present . . . Because its every ticking sound . . . Would make my life unpleasant . . . It would remind me constantly . . . How far I am behind . . . According to the schedule of . . . The work I have in mind . . . It would be like a monster that . . . Would never let me slumber . . . And when I have a job to do . . . It would report my number . . . I do not want a watch or clock . . . To tell the time of day . . . For it would only stretch my work . . . And shorten time for play . . . Just let me keep my record of . . . The minutes that are mounting . . . And then let God review my books . . . And do His own accounting.

MONDAY FOOTBALL

Monday is postmortem time . . . For Monday quarterbacks . . . The ones who just ignore each score . . . And tell you all the facts . . . About that certain touchdown that . . . Was fair as it could be . . . Though it was quickly canceled by . . . The stupid referee . . . The lowdown, dirty tactics that . . . The other team employed . . . And thus a perfect record for . . . The season was destroyed . . . The brilliant Monday quarterbacks . . . Who never played a game . . . And probably no other way . . . Have any claim to fame . . . But who are always experts and . . . Who would reverse the score . . . As football is their specialty . . . And they know so much more.

DEAR SON AND WIFE

God bless you, Jimmy, and God bless . . . Dear Beverly, your wife . . . And may you have a lasting and . . . A happy married life . . . We love you, son, our first-born child . . . And now especially too . . . Because it seems you chose the girl . . . Who was just right for you . . . We had been hoping for this day . . . And praying it would be . . . The kind that would bestow real joy . . . On all our family . . . And now we hope that you will have . . . A boy or girl someday . . . Who looks like you and Beverly . . . In every charming way . . . And when that baby comes along . . . you may be sure of it . . . Grandma dear and Grandpa will . . . Be glad to baby-sit.

NOTHING TO HIDE

Always to you my life, dear one . . . Will be an open book . . .
Where you will be most welcome, love . . . At any time to look . . .
Where you may see what I have done . . . Not just throughout this
day . . . But also all the months and years . . . That now are gone
away . . . There is not any thought or word . . . Or silent way I feel
. . . That I would try or even wish . . . To cover or conceal . . . Because my heart is confident . . . There is not any shame . . . That
could by any truthful means . . . Be fastened to my name . . . And
if you take that open book . . . And read the pages through . . .
They will reveal the only one . . . I ever loved—is you.

ON HIS OWN

A few short weeks ago in school . . . Your youngster started out
. . . To learn to read and write and what . . . This world is all about
. . . You thought he was a baby still . . . So helpless and so small
. . . You wanted to protect him with . . . Your warm, maternal
shawl . . . But now he looks so eager and . . . He has so much to
say . . . As he is growing wiser in . . . So many ways each day . . .
Not only does he march ahead . . . And take all things in stride
. . . His every manner indicates . . . His confidence and pride . . .
So do not worry any more . . . Though you may feel alone . . . If
he is to succeed in life . . . He must be on his own.

WHO SERVED IN WAR

Today we honor everyone . . . With prayer and praises warm . . .
Who served in time of battle in . . . A U.S. uniform . . . Especially each hero great . . . Who sleeps beneath a cross . . . Who
helped to bring us victory . . . But who became our loss . . . We
pray for them and praise them, and . . . Our hearts go out today
. . . To all the living veterans . . . Who served in any way . . . No
valuables upon this earth . . . Could ever pay the price . . . Of
their true patriotism and . . . Their noble sacrifice . . . We thank
them and salute them, and . . . May God forever bless . . . Each
one who wore in any war . . . Our military dress.

OUR SKY CAN CHANGE

When things go wrong at early dawn . . . It does not mean that we . . . Are doomed to spend the live-long day . . . In abject misery . . . The weather forecast may be bad . . . With skies quite overcast . . . And yet there always is a chance . . . The sun will shine at last . . . So in our lives the day may change . . . With prospects ever brighter . . . And gradually as hours pass . . . Our hearts may grow much lighter . . . But we must strive with all our might . . . To make this dream come true . . . By being cheerful in our thoughts . . . And all we say and do . . . It may seem very difficult . . . When things at first go wrong . . . But it is possible to turn . . . A tear into a song.

DAY JESUS DIED

This is the day in history . . . Our Lord and Saviour died . . . With nails through hands and feet, and with . . . A lance-wound in His side . . . The day when Jesus hung upon . . . The cross on Calvary . . . To expiate the countless sins . . . Of all humanity . . . Redeeming those whose hearts repent . . . The wrongs that they have done . . . The sins against almighty God . . . And His beloved Son . . . It is Good Friday all throughout . . . The Christian world today . . . A time to beg forgiveness, and . . . In silence bow and pray . . . So let us now be sorry for . . . The sins that are our own . . . And through a virtuous way of life . . . Endeavor to atone.

HAPPY HALLOWEEN

Halloween is really fun . . . For youngsters everywhere . . . Staying up and watching out . . . For witches in the air . . . Wearing costumes, playing games . . . At home or in the street . . . Ringing friendly doorbells, and . . . Exclaiming, "Trick or treat!" . . . Jack-o'-lanterns all around . . . Ghosts and devils cute . . . Giggling quite familiarly . . . To gather in their loot . . . It is all in healthy fun . . . As children like to play . . . If they cause no damage as . . . They go their merry way . . . Help them have a happy time . . . And give them something nice . . . You will find that it is worth . . . A hundred times the price.

OUR DREAM SHIP

Promise me that you will be . . . My own for evermore . . . For if
you do, my dream ship will . . . Be coming in to shore . . . A
dream ship filled with treasures from . . . Across the ocean blue . . .
Beautiful and wonderful . . . Though not as much as you . . .
All that magic will be yours . . . And I will be your own . . . And
you will be my only one . . . My only one, alone . . . Promise you
will love me in . . . Whatever storm or breeze . . . So we may board
our ship of dreams . . . And sail the seven seas . . . And then it
will not matter if . . . We never touch a shore . . . The two of us
together and . . . In love for evermore.

HEART OF A CITY

A city's heart is not downtown . . . However much it teems . . .
With business and excitement and . . . With all its civic dreams
. . . It is not in the City Hall . . . However great or good . . . But
in the common pulse that beats . . . In every neighborhood . . .
The heart of every city is . . . The people who are in it . . . Including those departed souls . . . Who labored to begin it . . . It
is the gossip on the street . . . The feeling at the polls . . . And all
the ones who volunteer . . . For patriotic roles . . . It is the taxes
that are paid . . . According to their worth . . . By residents who
would not take . . . Another place on earth.

WHATEVER YOU NEED

You know you have a friend in me . . . Wherever you may go . . .
So, please, do get in touch with me . . . When troubles seem to
grow . . . True friendship is a feeling of . . . The human mind and
heart . . . It is the soul of brotherhood . . . Never to be apart . . .
If you were tossed upon the sea . . . In stormiest of weather . . .
Although apart in body, we . . . Would carry on together . . . For
I would pray to God, and I . . . Am sure that He would hear . . .
And He would grant a miracle . . . To overcome your fear . . . So,
please, depend on me, my friend . . . And do not hesitate . . . To
ask for anything you need . . . However small or great.

DON'T FIGHT IT OUT

When you get in an argument . . . Though you may rage and shout
. . . Do not insist upon your fist . . . To try to fight it out . . . And
do not dare opponents to . . . Bet money then and there . . . To
settle any differences . . . Of who, what, when or where . . . No
fist can finally resolve . . . Who might be right in it . . . No blow,
however hard, can change . . . Opinions opposite . . . And do not
gamble money on . . . How smart you think yourself . . . You just
might lose your shirt and all . . . The groceries on your shelf . . .
A friendly little quarrel and . . . A wager made in fun . . . Are quite
all right, but don't get mad . . . In battles to be won.

GOD WILL REWARD US

God knows our heart's desires and . . . He answers every prayer . . .
If faithfully we strive to live . . . With caution and with care . . .
If we obey His holy will . . . On earth from day to day . . . By being good and doing good . . . In every humble way . . . As we respect our neighbor and . . . We practice charity . . . God will reward our efforts and . . . Protect our family . . . For that is all He
asks of us . . . To prove our mortal worth . . . As every sacrifice we
make . . . Will honor Him on earth . . . God loves us all, and
promises . . . That He will always bless . . . Each faithful soul with
all the best . . . Of health and happiness.

DEAR JIMMIE

Our heartfelt wishes, Jimmie, now . . . That you are twenty-two
. . . May all the best of health and wealth . . . And luck belong to
you . . . We are so proud of you today . . . Your mother dear and
I . . . Your brother and your sister too . . . That we just smile and
sigh . . . Your service in the Navy and . . . Your character so strong
. . . And all your efforts to be good . . . And prove that you belong
. . . Yes, you belong in every way . . . That any son could claim . . .
And I am proud especially . . . Because you bear my name . . . Con-
gratulations, Jimmie dear . . . And may this birthday be . . . Just
one of many more with joy . . . For all our family.

OUR FLOWER OF LOVE

Love is something beautiful . . . And love is something sweet . . .
And, like a flower has its seed . . . It starts when people meet . . .
And there it takes its roots, and then . . . It gradually will grow
. . . Until at last it blossoms, and . . . The lovers really know . . .
And that is how it all began . . . When first we met, my dear . . .
And how eventually our love . . . Became a bloom sincere . . .
Our love was planted when we met . . . And then the seed just
grew . . . Our friendship flowered into love . . . Our sweetest
dream came true . . . And now our love has blossomed, dear . . .
And it is ours to share . . . So let us always treat it with . . . The
tenderest of care.

HOSPITAL

It is not just a building that . . . Is made of stone or brick . . . A
place where you get expert help . . . When you are very sick . . .
The walls reflect devotion, with . . . A friendly roof above . . .
The floors are paths for feet that walk . . . With mercy and with
love . . . It is your temporary home . . . To guide you through a
spell . . . Of illness that is serious . . . And help you to get well . . .
Indeed it is a palace that . . . Provides the best of care . . . With
smiles and friendly greetings as . . . Your constant bill of fare . . .
And so when you must go there to . . . Preserve your life, or rest . . .
Remember always that you are . . . A very special guest.

PRIVATE PROBLEMS

Marriage problems are perhaps . . . The commonest of all . . . And
not uncommonly they shape . . . A tight and solid wall . . . As there
are certain marriages . . . That simply cannot last . . . Because of
present circumstance . . . Or something in the past . . . But many
are the problems that . . . Would never be so great . . . If gossips
did not spread the news . . . To every town and state . . . Prejudice
and jealousy . . . Ambition to be "smart" . . . Can wreck more
homes, as they prevent . . . The healing of a heart . . . The problems of a husband and . . . A wife should be their own . . . And
life would hold more happiness . . . If they were left alone.

TRAVEL TO LEARN

If now you plan to take a trip . . . At home or overseas . . . Be sure
that you bring back with you . . . Some worth-while memories . . .
Observe historic places, and . . . Acquire knowledge true . . . Which
someday may turn out to be . . . Invaluable to you . . . Don't
travel just to have some fun . . . By whiling time away . . . But
make it an intelligent . . . And useful holiday . . . Take in as many
of the sights . . . As you have time to see . . . You may not be so
blest again . . . With opportunity . . . Buy all the souvenirs and
things . . . You want to keep or give . . . But try to learn a little of
. . . How other people live.

OUR COLUMBUS

Some years I take my pen and write . . . About Columbus Day
. . . Though there are many folks who doubt . . . He ever came
this way . . . But if we study history . . . Our hearts will understand . . . That Christopher discovered what . . . Is now our famous land . . . He bartered with the Indians . . . And took some
back with him . . . Along with other treasures in . . . His hour
dark and dim . . . He did not win a fortune and . . . He made no
golden gains . . . Indeed he died a prisoner . . . Surrounded by
his chains . . . But he is our Columbus now . . . To me as well
as you . . . Who found this wondrous land of ours . . . In 1492.

ZOO KEEPER

The keeper of the zoo is one . . . Whose job it is to care . . . For
birds and animals inside . . . And in the open air . . . He has to
feed and tend to them . . . In every perfect way . . . And then
watch over all of them . . . When they are on display . . . A keeper
does his task quite well . . . As he maintains that score . . . But if
he really loves his job . . . He does a whole lot more . . . He trains
the inmates to perform . . . And guides the children through . . .
Explaining what they are and why . . . They act the way they do
. . . His wage may not be equal to . . . The sum that he is worth
. . . But God must love the joy he brings . . . To boys and girls on
earth.

OUR WINTERTIME

Of course I love you every day . . . And well you know it too . . .
But wintertime I set aside . . . Especially for you . . . For winter
is that season when . . . The snow is on the trees . . . And blaz-
ing logs bring back to life . . . Our dearest memories . . . The
shadows on the ceiling and . . . The glow upon the floor . . . And
you and I embraced in dreams . . . Of love forevermore . . . The
wind could shriek, the walls could shake . . . Until the dawn of day
. . . But all the strife and storm of life . . . Would swiftly melt
away . . . You in my arms, and I in yours . . . The bridegroom and
the bride . . . Nestled before the fireplace . . . With all the world
outside.

GOD'S LOVE FOR US

God's love for us is infinite . . . Far more than we deserve . . . He
loves us all, however well . . . Or poorly we may serve . . . He
loves us when we keep His word . . . With heart and spirit true
. . . Or if, to meet the public's gaze . . . We just pretend we do . . .
Yes, even when we turn away . . . And we deny His name . . .
However sinful we may be . . . His love remains the same . . . As
long as there is any chance . . . That we will be contrite . . . And
any hope that we will change . . . To doing what is right . . .
But sometime, somehow we must show . . . That we appreciate
. . . God's love for us so infinite . . . Before it is too late.

FRIENDLY INVITE

That phone call is a blessing when . . . A friend is ringing you . . .
And asks if there is anything . . . You really have to do . . . Or do
you have the time to spare . . . To spend an evening gay . . . With
relaxation truly good . . . To help you on your way? . . . It is the
phone call wonderful . . . That is a nice surprise . . . Just when
you are too tired to . . . Get up and exercise . . . And that is when
it really pays . . . To have that friend so true . . . Who really loves
you and who wants . . . To be of help to you . . . That phone call
is so marvelous . . . Just when you need it most . . . It makes you
deeply grateful to . . . Your gracious, timely host.

USEFUL MEMORIES

Memories are meaningful . . . And they are useful too . . . If they
are really beautiful . . . And they inspire you . . . Memories of
childhood and . . . Of friendships that were sweet . . . Wound
around the happiness . . . Of some familiar street . . . Shadows
in the sunlight that . . . Were fairies in a dream . . . With stronger
strokes in swimming on . . . Through life's engulfing stream . . .
But not if you would run away . . . To live those days again . . .
For nothing can ever be . . . The same as it was then . . . The
only worthwhile memories . . . Are those that light your dawn . . .
With happiness, devotion and . . . The courage to go on.

NAPKIN

The napkin is protection for . . . The one with manners sloppy
. . . And demonstrates to younger folks . . . Who otherwise might
copy . . . It shows how useful it can be . . . When you are slurping
soup . . . Or sipping gravy with a fork . . . Alone or in a group
. . . The napkin guards against the need . . . For cleaning and
for pressing . . . As you may fumble the dessert . . . The cream
or salad dressing . . . Of course there are some people quaint . . .
Who never make a slip . . . And use the cloth or paper kind . . .
To sort of pat the lip . . . But any way you look at it . . . The napkin gives protection . . . And when your manners are at stake . . .
It helps you pass inspection.

DON IS IN LOVE

We got a real cute letter from . . . Our youngest son today . . . A
law school junior, 22 . . . Who had these words to say . . . "Dear
Mother and dear Daddy, it . . . Is really spring for me . . . For I
am just as much in love . . . As anyone can be" . . . Don told
us all about the girl . . . So beautiful and sweet . . . And said he
hoped before too long . . . His darling we would meet . . . And
then he gave assurance that . . . He did not have in mind . . . A
hasty flight from bacherlorhood . . . To wedding vows that bind
. . . "Marriage right away is not . . . What I am thinking of . . .
But it is springtime, and it sure . . . Is nice to be in love."

WANT-AD FOR YOU

I buy the paper every day . . . And read the want-ads through . . .
For that small possibility . . . That I appeal to you . . . I mean the
ads called "Personal" . . . Where you might call to me . . . With
printed words and phrases to . . . Arouse my memory . . . But
never any ad appears . . . To give me any trace . . . Of where I
now could find you, dear . . . In any certain place . . . And so I
send this message in . . . A want-ad of my own . . . That I am so
in love with you . . . And want just you alone . . . I hope you see
my ad among . . . The "Personals" you read . . . And answer fa-
vorably, my dear . . . The loving cause I plead.

APPOINTMENTS

Appointments in the business world . . . Are those we have to keep
. . . And they allow no time for us . . . To doze or oversleep . . . Our
time is regulated by . . . The dates that we have made . . . And just
the thought of breaking one . . . Makes most of us afraid . . . And
yet how real important are . . . Appointments after all? . . . And
what would happen if we failed . . . To make a certain call? . . . And
how do they compare with those . . . We ought to keep each day . . .
As we have promised God that we . . . Will take some time to pray?
. . . Appointments are important but . . . Our failure to appear . . .
Should always be entitled to . . . An explanation clear.

NO PAGE IS WASTED

In school we studied literature . . . Poetic plays and such . . . And for
the larger part of it . . . We did not care so much . . . It seemed so
useless on our way . . . To earn a livelihood . . . That we were puz-
zled as to how . . . It could do any good . . . But as the years went
by, we learned . . . Those hours were not wasted . . . Not even if
that culture was . . . A dish we only tasted . . . Somehow it helped
the grammar of . . . Our vocal chords and pen . . . And there were
famous passages . . . We quoted now and then . . . The classics are
no guarantee . . . Of ultimate success . . . But they can guide the
intellect . . . To greater happiness.

NOT STRANGE AT ALL

Have you approached a certain place . . . Or knocked upon a door
. . . Where you were really certain you . . . Had never been before
. . . And yet you had the feeling that . . . Sometime you had been
there . . . And when you struggled to recall . . . It vanished into air?
. . . Or have you ever met someone . . . Whose name was new to
you . . . But who in some vague manner seemed . . . Like somebody
you knew? . . . It is a vision weird that comes . . . Upon you now
and then . . . As though you had been born before . . . And you
were here again . . . It is a strange reaction, but . . . Don't let it
worry you . . . For it is just a fantasy . . . Most normal minds go
through.

GIVE US A MIRROR, GOD

Give us a mirror, God, that will . . . Reflect our frailty . . . Of finding fault with other souls . . . In our community . . . A looking glass
that will reveal . . . The sins that weigh us down . . . Beyond the
right to criticize . . . The neighbors in our town . . . And all our
neighbors everywhere . . . Throughout the world You made . . . As
we should never praise ourselves . . . For any higher grade . . . Give
us a mirror, God, to see . . . How wrong we really are . . . To sit in
moral judgment on . . . Each other, near or far . . . A mirror, God,
that will reflect . . . The sins that are our own . . . And why we
have no right to cast . . . The very smallest stone.

HELP CRIPPLED KIDS

Consider in your charity . . . The little girls and boys . . . Who do
not have the strength to share . . . In other children's joys . . . The
ones who cannot walk or run . . . Or jump around in glee . . . And
who must live without the hope . . . Of full recovery . . . Who will
be grateful for your aid . . . To soothe their suffering . . . And for the
added courage that . . . Your offering will bring . . . They do not
make their own appeal . . . And they do not complain . . . However dark the outlook, and . . . However long the rain . . . Do buy
some Easter seals today . . . Give all you can afford . . . God's blessing and your happy heart . . . Will be your rich reward.

WE TWO FOREVER

Your smiles are all my happiness . . . Your sorrows are my tears . . .
And every word you whisper, love . . . Will linger through the years
. . . I cherish every song you sing . . . Each sentiment and sigh . . .
And when you slip your hand in mine . . . I know the reason why
. . . I know you care for me as much . . . As I belong to you . . .
And to the end of life our love . . . Will be forever true . . . No mat-
ter where we roam this earth . . . However far apart . . . I shall be
yours, and you will be . . . Forever in my heart . . . And so our
promise will endure . . . For all the time we live . . . With everything that you bestow . . . And all that I can give.

FRIENDLY TALK

A friendly talk is one good way . . . To rest and to relax . . . With
words about the future or . . . Some past or present facts . . . It is a
good thing to exchange . . . The knowledge we possess . . . Especially philosophy . . . And dreams of happiness . . . So many times
we get ideas . . . We never would have known . . . Had we main-
tained a silent tongue . . . And walked our way alone . . . A friendly
talk can wake us up . . . Arouse our energies . . . And thus prevent
our missing out . . . On opportunities . . . It can be just a pleasant
means . . . For rest and relaxation . . . But sometimes even idle
words . . . Bring fruitful inspiration.

NO EMPTY HOUSE

No house is ever empty if . . . You really look around . . . Where
once a family has lived . . . Though now there is no sound . . . There
are those marks upon the walls . . . And scratches on each chair . . .
Or other signs that children once . . . Were loved and cared for there
. . . And as you go from room to room . . . Around that silent place
. . . You seem to sense their laughter, and . . . You see each little
face . . . No house is ever empty where . . . A family has dwelt . . .
As much as memories remain . . . Of love so dearly felt . . . There
may be nobody inside . . . But you will be aware . . . Of ghosts that
will inform you of . . . The joy that once was there.

NO LUCK IN LIFE

There's no such thing as luck in life . . . As some of us believe . . .
That by some strange coincidence . . . We fail or we achieve . . .
There is no four-leaf clover or . . . A horseshoe on the wall . . . Or
any rabbit's foot or sign . . . That helps us out at all . . . Yes, there
is such a word as "luck" . . . But it is meant to say . . . The fortune
good or bad that we . . . Experience every day . . . Not any turning
of the tide . . . That conjures up the breaks . . . But our successful
efforts or . . . Our commonplace mistakes . . . Whatever happens in
this life . . . It should not seem so odd . . . Somehow we are to
blame or it . . . Is by the will of God.

OUR HELP TO THEM

Presumably our two big boys . . . Are gathering some knowledge
. . . As they pursue their studies in . . . Their higher years of college
. . . But all the evidence we have . . . Of things they really learn . . .
Is that they think they have it made . . . With nothing they must
earn . . . They figure they can sponge on us . . . Not even wash the
dishes . . . And somehow Dad and Mommy will . . . Fulfill their
slightest wishes . . . But it will not be long before . . . They get a
great surprise . . . As we remind them of their debt . . . And cut
them down to size . . . And when they reach the platform to . . .
Receive that dear diploma . . . We hope that they will recognize . . .
That discipline aroma.

CARTOONS

Cartoons can be real funny, and . . . They can be caustic too . . .
And sometimes they reflect the thoughts . . . That others think of
you . . . They help to editorialize . . . The topic of the day . . . Or
simply serve to entertain . . . And pass the time away . . . They are
the mental pictures that . . . Adorn the drawing board . . . To fill up
space or take their place . . . In winning some award . . . Cartoons
can be quite beautiful . . . Or just a sorry sight . . . According to
the artist's view . . . Of what is wrong and right . . . But whether
they are cheaply made . . . Or they involve expense . . . Cartoons
are just a waste of time . . . Unless they make some sense.

MEETING A MUTT

You move into a neighborhood . . . That is so new to you . . . Not
just the people all around . . . But all the canines too . . . The poodle
that knows only French . . . The collie soft and kind . . . A dachshund like our Pretzel and . . . All breeds that you can find . . . So
many of them bark and look . . . As though they want to bite . . . It
makes you wonder if you can . . . Get in your house all right . . .
But you can solve that problem well . . . However late you came
. . . By simply finding out from folks . . . The canine's calling name
. . . Then if it ever threatens you . . . Just call its name out loud . . .
The dog will be obedient . . . And you will be quite proud.

NOSTALGIA

Nostalgia is any scene . . . Wherever you may roam . . . That makes
you wish with all your heart . . . That you could be back home . . .
It is a song of long ago . . . That interrupts your schemes . . . And
magically withdraws you to . . . Your world of youthful dreams . . .
Or it may be a sudden voice . . . Or some familiar face . . . You feel
that you remember, yet . . . Somehow you cannot place . . . Nostalgia is sentiment . . . Created by the past . . . But it is made of
gossamer . . . And therefore cannot last . . . It is a ghost that haunts
your mind . . . If only for a while . . . To change your frowning
features to . . . A sentimental smile.

MAYBE—I DOUBT IT

I doubt if you remember me . . . But even if you do . . . Your heart
will never know how much . . . I really thought of you . . . Because
I never told you and . . . I could not say it now . . . That heaven
would be mine if we . . . Exchanged the marriage vow . . . And if
somehow my thoughts could find . . . Your street address today . . .
I wonder if you would believe . . . The words I want to say . . . The
chances are that you have reached . . . A brighter, better dawn . . .
And you have every reason to . . . Be glad that I am gone . . . But if
it still is possible . . . That you believe in me . . . I will belong to
you, my love . . . For all eternity.

GOD BLESSES LOVE

God loves each valentine on earth . . . From one heart to another . . . From sister, brother, sweetheart, friend . . . And every dad and mother . . . For God designed and He ordained . . . That love should always be . . . Our bond with Him, our neighbor and . . . With all humanity . . . Each valentine—a card or gift . . . Or just a fond hello . . . By phone or telegram becomes . . . A blessing we bestow . . . What message can be sweeter than . . . A gentle valentine? . . . "I love you, dear, with all my heart . . . Please, be forever mine" . . . And as we mean and we fulfill . . . The love we are expressing . . . We may be certain that our hearts . . . Will gain God's richest blessing.

CHEERLEADER

With multiple gyrations and . . . A voice astonishing . . . He strives to rouse a stadium . . . Or make the rafters ring . . . In college or in high school, he . . . Commands the students' tiers . . . As he jumps up and leads them in . . . Their unison of cheers . . . He may seem somewhat funny, or . . . That "he" may be a gal . . . But anyone who draws those cheers . . . Is boosting school morale . . . Cheerleaders are a specialty . . . As much as those who play . . . And now and then they are the ones . . . Who really save the day . . . In football, baseball, basketball . . . In hockey or the track . . . Let's give each good cheerleader now . . . A pat upon the back.

WITH FAITH IN GOD

This is our day in history . . . The fourth day of July . . . Let us do honor to our flag . . . As it goes marching by . . . Let us remove our hats, and place . . . The hand upon the breast . . . With thanks to God for liberty . . . With which we have been blest . . . The stars and stripes are on parade . . . Our nation celebrates . . . The freedom we have always had . . . In our United States . . . There have been wars, and many are . . . Our military dead . . . And always we are threatened by . . . Another fight ahead . . . But as our only aim is peace . . . We raise our flag with pride . . . And we have faith and confidence . . . That God is on our side.

41

A WEE BIT BETTER

Through all the days and weeks and months . . . That I have known
you, dear . . . Each moment has convinced me more . . . That you
are so sincere . . . I could not ever doubt you in . . . The very smallest way . . . And, oh, that fills my heart with joy . . . My dearest,
every day . . . I thank you for the promise of . . . Your love forever
true . . . And in return I give myself . . . Forevermore to you . . .
Our bargain seems an equal one . . . And yet that is not so . . .
As there is bound to be some more . . . That I will always owe . . .
Though both of us are equal to . . . The final human letter . . . I
do believe, my dearest one . . . You are a wee bit better.

FRIENDS NEXT DOOR

We cannot have too many friends . . . If they are tried and true . . .
But in that category they . . . Are usually quite few . . . Of those
we meet from day to day . . . So many disappear . . . As they are
simply transient or . . . We find them insincere . . . It would be
wonderful if all . . . The charming folks we meet . . . Could be as
close and permanent . . . As neighbors on our street . . . Of course
not everyone of those . . . Is perfect in the sun . . . But we would
settle any day . . . Upon the average one . . . Because the neighbors
that we have . . . However old or new . . . Befriend us in emergen-
cies . . . Which proves that they are true.

TOPSY-TURVY

It is a topsy-turvy world . . . When you consider it . . . A sort of jigsaw puzzle with . . . The pieces hard to fit . . . The children want to
be grown up . . . They make like Mom and Dad . . . As they play
house, and they pretend . . . Their kids are good or bad . . . And
when the years go by and when . . . They raise a family . . . They
sigh because they have so much . . . Responsibility . . . They wish,
if only for a day . . . They could be small again . . . As carefree and
protected and . . . As gay as they were then . . . Until at last the
jigsaw fades . . . When all the pieces fit . . . As now they realize they
are grown . . . And they are stuck with it.

RESCUE WORK

Rescue work is noble work . . . That calls for bravery . . . To help a human life survive . . . In time of tragedy . . . A dangerous assignment that . . . Requires heart and mind . . . And more than any other thing . . . The wisdom to be kind . . . In many cases rescue work . . . Is strictly voluntary . . . Regardless of the risk involved . . . Real or imaginary . . . Without the slightest thought of praise . . . Or any special prize . . . But just the hope instinctive that . . . No injured person dies . . . And when the rescue worker has . . . To pay the final price . . . He has God's promise that there is . . . No greater sacrifice.

JOYFUL JOURNEY

God bless you and protect you as . . . You journey on your way . . . And may His loving hand reach forth . . . To guide you night and day . . . May every turning of the road . . . Reveal a brighter view . . . With everything of friendliness . . . And happiness for you . . . Wherever you may linger, may . . . You be the privileged guest . . . Enjoying food and drink and all . . . The comforts of the best . . . May every place you visit and . . . Each smiling face you see . . . Become a pleasant picture in . . . Your lifelong memory . . . And when you reach the point where you . . . Decide to turn around . . . God grant your journey home will be . . . Serene and safe and sound.

FORGETFUL PARKING

Professors may declare they are . . . Forever in distress . . . But they have no monopoly . . . On absent-mindedness . . . For there was that occasion when . . . My daughter dear and I . . . Drove into town to look around . . . And see what we could buy . . . We parked the car in some garage . . . And went along our way . . . And finally concluded our . . . Delightful shopping day . . . But we were so accustomed to . . . A ride upon the bus . . . That having left the car downtown . . . Did not occur to us . . . Until we both were home again . . . And saw her mommy's frown . . . Then Kris and I recalled the car . . . And hurried back to town.

ALL I EXPECT

How much do I expect from you . . . As we together live? . . . No
more than I am able, dear . . . In my poor way to give . . . Indeed
there is not anything . . . That I expect from you . . . Except that
every day and night . . . You will be really true . . . I do not ask your
sympathy . . . Or understanding tone . . . And I can stand the loneliness . . . When I must be alone . . . I do not mind if I give more
. . . Than you may offer me . . . As I would have your heart rejoice
. . . In every memory . . . The only thing that I expect . . . The
same as from a friend . . . Is that you will be faithful, dear . . .
Unto the very end.

CITY AT NIGHT

I like the large metropolis . . . Especially at night . . . When boulevards and buildings tall . . . Are bathed in gleaming light . . . The
theaters and studios . . . Hotels and quaint cafés . . . The taxicabs
and private cars . . . That flow in endless maze . . . And all the
people everywhere . . . Who stroll or hurry by . . . Beneath the
mirror of a moon . . . And stars around the sky . . . I feel the racing
pulse of life . . . And suddenly I seem . . . To wander in a wonderland . . . Surrounded by a dream . . . Until the lights are going out
. . . And shadows take the places . . . Of human forms that filled
the street . . . With bright and happy faces.

FREE LANCE

A free lance is a person who . . . Is strictly on his own . . . Who
looks around for business, and . . . Who handles it alone . . . Who
has no boss to shout at him . . . And tell him what to do . . . But
who decides things for himself . . . To see each project through . . .
It may seem very wonderful . . . And quite a life of ease . . . But
every customer he gets . . . Is one he has to please . . . Some days he
gets no coffee break . . . His time is never free . . . Each undertaking
is his sole . . . Responsibility . . . The free lance who succeeds in
life . . . Has really got it made . . . But it is quite a gamble, and . . .
Not many make the grade.

44

TYLER IS HAPPY

When little Tyler came on earth . . . It made his parents sad . . .
Because his right arm was deformed . . . And it looked somewhat
bad . . . Their thoughts were not concerned with pride . . . But with
a future dim . . . As Tyler's strange condition might . . . Become a
shock to him . . . That happened four long years ago . . . Today they
need not fear . . . As he is taking life in stride . . . With all the best
of cheer . . . He saw a little, crippled girl . . . Who could not walk
or run . . . And so was obviously denied . . . Much normal, healthy
fun . . . His handicap disturbs him not . . . As some might stare or
scoff . . . He realizes in many ways . . . He could have been worse
off.

LET ME SERVE YOU

I know, my Lord and God, with all . . . The virtues that I lack . . .
There is no way upon this earth . . . That I could pay You back . . .
That I could reimburse You, God . . . For my immortal soul
. . . And for the chance I have to reach . . . That great, eternal goal
. . . But I am grateful for my life . . . In all humility . . . And beg
You for Your loving grace . . . To help inspire me . . . That I may
be of service in . . . The smallest way at all . . . And thereby do the
least I can . . . Whenever You may call . . . Just let me be Your serv-
ant, Lord . . . In any way I can . . . As I may lend a helping hand
. . . Unto some fellow man.

PEACE AT HOME

I like to meet a special friend . . . And chat with him at length . . .
About the problems of this life . . . Our weakness and our strength
. . . To learn his views on questions that . . . Confront the world
today . . . And so much more the little ones . . . Along our local way
. . . The difficulties that we meet . . . And sometimes get us down
. . . In school and business, neighborhood . . . And all around the
town . . . I think the little problems of . . . This life mean so much
more . . . And personal togetherness . . . Could put an end to war
. . . Small problems solve the large ones and . . . We could defeat
the devil . . . If we would all be tolerant . . . Upon the local level.

I WANT YOUR HEART

You said you would not marry me . . . Because you were not fair
. . . And in your heart you were convinced . . . I did not really care
. . . You thought that you were homely and . . . I'd think the same
of you . . . And even if I gave my pledge . . . I never would be true
. . . But you are beautiful to me . . . Believe me, I adore you . . .
And there is nothing in this world . . . That I would not do for you
. . . To me you are the answer to . . . My every hope and prayer . . .
The only one for whom my heart . . . Could ever really care . . . I
think you're beautiful, but looks . . . Are no important part . . . The
only thing I really want . . . Is just your loving heart.

I WISH MORE OFTEN

I wish I had a magic way . . . To keep in constant touch . . . With
all my friends who are so kind . . . And mean so very much . . . But
they and I are occupied . . . With many things each day . . . There
seldom is a brief hello . . . That we have time to say . . . When we
can get together, we . . . Are happy as can be . . . And it is wonderful to have . . . Such friendly company . . . And so the best that
I can do . . . Is see them now and then . . . And tell each one I hope
real soon . . . We two shall meet again . . . But I am overjoyed because . . . My friendships are so many . . . How lonely my poor
heart would be . . . If now I had not any!

NO LEARNING LOST

That time is never wasted in . . . Scholastic atmosphere . . . Which
is intended to prepare . . . For some worth while career . . . For even
if we lack the means . . . Or opportunity . . . To carry out the aim of
what . . . We hope to do or be . . . The knowledge that we gather
will . . . Be helpful in some way . . . However indirectly, to . . . Our
progress of the day . . . For nothing that we learn is lost . . . To be of
no avail . . . If we keep trying faithfully . . . Determined not to fail
. . . And always it is possible . . . Our tide of life will turn . . . And
perseverance will attain . . . The goal for which we yearn.

REAL TEAMWORK

Teamwork is not tailored for . . . The world of sports alone . . . It is
intended daily for . . . The young as well as grown . . . It is the measure of a man . . . Who does not reach for fame . . . But who is only
interested . . . In helping win the game . . . By working for a charity
. . . Or some good civic cause . . . Without the least desire for . . .
A trophy or applause . . . A fine example is the one . . . Who sacrifices rest . . . To turn out scripts for local shows . . . To help them
be the best . . . If they reject his efforts, he . . . Can still have happiness . . . For having played upon the team . . . To make it a success.

GOD'S GREATEST GIFT

The little town of Bethlehem . . . Is peacefully asleep . . . While
shepherds on the hills beyond . . . Are tending to their sheep . . .
There is a whisper in the wind . . . Of angels in the sky . . . And suddenly a brilliant star . . . Is visible on high . . . The heavens seem to
open wide . . . Angelic voices sing . . . And wonderful and joyful
are . . . The tidings that they bring . . . The Baby Jesus, Son of God
. . . In Bethlehem is born . . . God's greatest gift to all on earth . . .
This glorious Christmas Morn . . . Let us rejoice and worship Him
. . . And let us humbly pray . . . For grace and guidance and the
strength . . . To live a better way.

RAISE IN PAY

A raise in pay does not depend . . . On miracles you do . . . But just
how well you serve your boss . . . And what he thinks of you . . . A
raise in pay depends upon . . . Your careful concentration . . . On
duties that are clerical . . . Or typing and dictation . . . Your prompt-
ness in the morning and . . . Your willingness to stay . . . A little late
when there is work . . . That should be cleared away . . . Your
attitude towards everyone . . . Your effort to be cheerful . . . And
keeping gossip to yourself . . . If you should get an earful . . . A raise
in pay must be deserved . . . By many things done well . . . And
being always eager to . . . Improve and to excel.

OUR SPECIAL BOND

There are special bonds we buy . . . To prosecute a war . . . And
those we purchase for defense . . . To guard our peaceful door . . .
There are those investment bonds . . . That gather interest high . . .
From real estate and buildings that . . . Would penetrate the sky . . .
But there has never been a bond . . . And there will never be . . . A
bond as precious as the one . . . That binds your heart to me . . .
Our bond of love in marriage, dear . . . As we are one today . . . The
special interest-bearing bond . . . Of work and sleep and play . . .
The kind of special interest that . . . Is not concerned with money
. . . But just the kind I have in you . . . Because you are my honey.

THIS IS THE TOWN

Of all the towns and cities, with . . . Their boulevards and trees . . .
This is the one that surely holds . . . My fondest memories . . . Each
time I visit here again . . . I dream back through the years . . . And
live again the hopes of youth . . . And all its smiles and tears . . . I
wander down the avenues . . . And touch remembered places . . .
As wistfully I look around . . . For some familiar faces . . . The
laughter and the heartaches now . . . Are faded far away . . . But I
still like to make believe . . . Today is yesterday . . . I know it cannot
come to life . . . The way it used to be . . . But, oh, I love the fairyland . . . Of timeless memory.

FOR YOU, OUR JIMMIE

Dear Jimmie, you are twenty-three . . . And we are happy son . . .
Because of all your progress and . . . The laurels you have won . . .
Your service in the navy and . . . Your constant search for knowledge . . . That soon will bring you to your goal . . . Of graduating
college . . . A happy birthday, Jimmie, and . . . The best of luck to
you . . . May all your prayers be well fulfilled . . . And all your
dreams come true . . . We wish you every great success . . . To which
you may aspire . . . And every other joy in life . . . You ever could
desire . . . We tell you every birthday but . . . This one of twenty-
three . . . Brings extra special greetings from . . . Your mother and
from me.

PUBLICITY HOUNDS

Some people will do anything . . . To get publicity . . . However bad
or fairly good . . . The notices may be . . . Their only interest is to
gain . . . Some great financial prize . . . Or make them look important far . . . Above their actual size . . . They do not care how false
or how . . . Exaggerated are . . . The stories and announcements of
. . . A genius or a star . . . They just want prominence in life . . .
To reach their selfish goals . . . Regardless of what damage they . . .
May do to other souls . . . They are the kind of people who . . .
Will traffic in deceit . . . To seize the smallest glory, but . . . Who
cannot take defeat.

GOD BLESS OUR WAY

Our Constitution is our crown . . . And it is the foundation . . . Of
all the principles in life . . . That dedicate our nation . . . It may
have different meanings, as . . . Our government sees fit . . . And
as the highest justices . . . Sometimes interpret it . . . But it is still
the document . . . That makes our children certain . . . That they
are always free and safe . . . From any kind of curtain . . . And so
we get together on . . . This Constitution Day . . . To make the
whole world conscious of . . . Our democratic way . . . It is our patriotic time . . . And common resolution . . . To ask God's blessing
on our land . . . And on our Constitution.

MAIL-CALL AT CAMP

One card or letter in the mail . . . One little postage stamp . . . Can
mean so much to boys and girls . . . Who are away at camp . . . It
may be seldom and not much . . . That they write back to you . . .
As they are making friends, and have . . . So many things to do . . .
Yet they experience loneliness . . . While others run and shout
. . . Especially at mail-time when . . . Their names are not called
out . . . You need not take the time each day . . . To write to her or
him . . . But just sufficient messages . . . To keep them in the
"swim" . . . Each note or little package is . . . A truly priceless gem
. . . As it is proof that somebody . . . Is really fond of them.

TO SEAL OUR VOW

Last night became a sacred night . . . As I proposed to you . . . And you accepted, darling, and . . . We promised to be true . . . So now we are engaged, my love . . . According to God's way . . . And I am looking forward to . . . Our wondrous wedding day . . . When I shall hold you in my arms . . . To love and keep forever . . . While offering with all my heart . . . My very least endeavor . . . I want to give you all of me . . . As I want all of you . . . That we may share our thoughts and words . . . And everything we do . . . God love you, darling, for your lips . . . So sweet and precious now . . . As they agreed last night, dear one . . . To seal our marriage vow.

ETERNAL FATHER

Eternal Father, loving God . . . Considerate and good . . . Bestow Your blessing on each soul . . . And every neighborhood . . . Give us the strength we need—let not . . . Our efforts be in vain . . . Help us to reach each worthy goal . . . We struggle to attain . . . Forgive our weakness and our sins . . . As we fall by the way . . . And give us courage to arise . . . And live a better day . . . Eternal Father, source of life . . . Our faith we now renew . . . All that we are and all we have . . . Are special gifts from You . . . We praise You and adore You and . . . We kneel before Your throne . . . Eternal God, without Whose grace . . . Man would be all alone.

I WISH YOU WELL

I always wish you well, my friend . . . Wherever you may be . . . Because each day in every way . . . You mean so much to me . . . I may not see you for a while . . . Or know just where you are . . . But you are in my fondest thoughts . . . However near or far . . . Your faithfulness and kindness give . . . That inspiration true . . . To live the hours of each day . . . A little more like you . . . I thank you most sincerely and . . . I hope the prayers I say . . . Will do at least a little good . . . To help you on your way . . . However seldom we may meet . . . With little time to spend . . . I think of you each moment and . . . I wish you well, my friend.

LEAST FORTUNATE

The children of the poor are those . . . Most fortunate today . . .
They know that they have nothing and . . . They have to work their
way . . . And so they struggle to support . . . Their parents and themselves . . . And they are always grateful for . . . The groceries on their
shelves . . . The children of the rich are next . . . If in their luxuries
. . . They do not laugh and toss aside . . . Their opportunities . . .
While last are those whose parents seem . . . To be quite well-to-do
. . . But actually cannot afford . . . Their car or castle new . . . They
are the children comfortable . . . Who cannot understand . . . Why
now and then their parents must . . . Refuse what they demand.

A WATCH

A watch is just an article . . . To tell the time of day . . . And help
you keep a certain date . . . Or quickly run away . . . Its hands are
not responsible . . . For what you have to do . . . But they will point
the hour out . . . That means so much to you . . . A watch is a re-
minder of . . . The promise that you made . . . And of how little
time is left . . . If now you are afraid . . . Or it may tick too slowly
as . . . You wait for sunny skies . . . If only from the lovelight of
. . . A certain pair of eyes . . . You set the hands and wind the stem
. . . But all a watch can do . . . Is just to run around its face . . .
And show the time to you.

TO RAISE A CHILD

It is not easy nowadays . . . To raise a child or two . . . And have
them be in every way . . . Obedient to you . . . Somehow it seems so
different from . . . The time when you were small . . . As you adjust
the picture of . . . The days that you recall . . . If only by some magic
wand . . . You now could take their place . . . You would remember
childhood and . . . The fears you had to face . . . You would remember clearly, and . . . You would appreciate . . . That sometimes children disobey . . . And sometimes they are late . . . You
would become more tolerant . . . And lend a gentle hand . . . As
lovingly and loyally . . . Your heart would understand.

BELIEVE IN ME

I know you think that I am young . . . Your parents think so too . . . But truly and sincerely, dear . . . I am in love with you . . . And maybe you are older by . . . A passing year or so . . . But that should make no difference in . . . The common world we know . . . Perhaps my chances of success . . . Just now are not so bright . . . But I have faith, my dear, as I . . . Am striving day and night . . . I mean to finish college and . . . Pursue a good career . . . And at this time your loving vow . . . Could help so much, my dear . . . Let's not divide the teardrops of . . . The trite and tedious play . . . Where boy makes good, and girl is sad . . . Because she walked away.

FOUR WINDS, AHOY!

Along about this time of year . . . Kristina starts to dream . . . Of Four Winds camp in Washington . . . And of her summer scheme . . . To see Deer Harbor once again . . . And all the friends she won . . . When they were walking through the woods . . . Or sailing in the sun . . . She dreams of happy voyages . . . And gay campfire songs . . . And all she really wants is just . . . To know that she belongs . . . But Kris does more than merely dream . . . She has her piggy banks . . . Where every contribution now . . . Receives her heartfelt thanks . . . And she is kissing Daddy for . . . A dollar now and then . . . So she can spend the summertime . . . At Four Winds camp again.

BROTHERS ALWAYS

This week reminds us all to live . . . As brothers in this life . . . To put away our differences . . . And to forget all strife . . . Because this week is set aside . . . For brotherhood on earth . . . When all of us should strive to be . . . Of more enduring worth . . . And that is good, but why should there . . . Be need of a campaign . . . at any time throughout the year . . . To make a further gain? . . . We should be brothers every day . . . In every way we can . . . As much as we are capable . . . To serve our fellowman . . . So let us keep this thought in mind . . . With charity and cheer . . . And live in brotherhood throughout . . . Each day of every year.

JUST SO MUCH TIME

Nothing can be permanent . . . As life goes on its way . . . There has to be a certain end . . . To every night and day . . . Hopes and fears, and joys and tears . . . Are only temporary . . . The same as relatives and friends . . . Someday the world must bury . . . So why should we succumb to fear . . . And let it grip the nation? . . . Or why should we endeavor to . . . Prolong a celebration? . . . Consider now the consequence . . . Of living to excess . . . We cannot regulate our time . . . Of tears or happiness . . . So why not just take life in stride . . . And keep our balance true . . . As God allows us time on earth . . . For what we try to do?

GIVE US YOUR GRACE

Give us, O God, the grace to live . . . A better life each day . . . In all our thoughts and all our deeds . . . And every word we say . . . Give us the courage that we need . . . To live a virtuous life . . . And not to be discouraged by . . . Distress or any strife . . . We want to serve you faithfully . . . With love and work and prayer . . . Especially by doing good . . . To neighbors everywhere . . . Let not our hearts be fearful in . . . The darkness of the night . . . But lead us gently to the dawn . . . Of hope and vision bright . . . And when we fall along the way . . . As we have done before . . . Forgive us our transgressions, God . . . And lift us up once more.

IT IS YOUR CASTLE

Your home is quite a castle, where . . . You have the only say . . . It is a fortress strong—at least . . . Most every legal way . . . It may not be a structure tall . . . That stands upon a hill . . . With turrets and a banner bright . . . At every window sill . . . It may be just a small abode . . . Along some avenue . . . That always is an open house . . . To those who call on you . . . But it is still your castle, and . . . No one may enter there . . . Without express permission, as . . . Your home you wish to share . . . No one may trespass on your land . . . And you are free to draw . . . Whatever weapon you may choose . . . Except against the law.

MY LIFE, MY ALL

You ask me, dearest one, how much . . . You really mean to me . . .
And I can only say you are . . . My life, my memory . . . You are
today, tomorrow, and . . . From New Year through December . . .
The only one I cherish and . . . I always would remember . . . My
life had little meaning, dear . . . Until you came along . . . And then
my heart was happy, and . . . The world became a song . . . And so
I measure time on earth . . . And every kind of weather . . . According to how long our hearts . . . Have really been together . . . And
as you love me day and night . . . I give my promise true . . . With
all my heart and all my soul . . . I do belong to you.

YOUR DOG

Your dog may have a pedigree . . . As far as records reach . . . And
it may be obedient . . . To everything you teach . . . Or it may be a
common mutt . . . That lingers at your feet . . . Because somewhere
it found you, as . . . You walked along the street . . . It may become
a champion . . . Or just a household pet . . . But if you love that
animal . . . It never will forget . . . For every pat you give it, and . . .
For every friendly smile . . . Your dog will cuddle up to you . . . And
follow you each mile . . . It will be truly loyal, and . . . Protect you
to the end . . . Yes, it will even die for you . . . To prove it is your
friend.

HONEST FRIEND

A friend is one who really should . . . Be always tried and true . . .
But do not ever ask of him . . . To tell a lie for you . . . He cannot
be your honest friend . . . And at the same time be . . . The one who
would defend you with . . . His own dishonesty . . . For if he does
not speak the truth . . . Whatever time or place . . . Eventually he
may bestow . . . A mutual disgrace . . . It is a faithless loyalty . . .
If it involves a lie . . . Yes, even when to save someone . . . Who is
about to die . . . No friend is ever worth your while . . . Unless his
tongue is true . . . To all the world with honest words . . . As he stand
up for you.

PIECE TO SPEAK

Furniture and bric-a-brac . . . Are pleasant to behold . . . Made of
wood or china or . . . Of silver, bronze or gold . . . But why is some
such item called . . . A conversation piece . . . As though, if it
should be removed . . . All talk would quickly cease? . . . Why
should we need a painting old . . . Or ornament unique . . . To
interest welcome callers and . . . Inspire them to speak? . . . Are we
so dull and stupid that . . . We feel ourselves quite lost . . . Without
some object that appears . . . To represent high cost? . . . The only
conversation piece . . . That is a work of art . . . Is that small piece
of friendship said . . . Sincerely from the heart.

LOVE YOU, PRETZEL

Happy birthday, Pretzel—you . . . Are six years old today . . . We
wish you many years to come . . . In which to run and play . . . You
are the dearest dachshund, so . . . Affectionate, sincere . . . With
stubby legs, and snout and tail . . . That stretch from there to here
. . . We know you're always hungry and . . . You sleep all day and
night . . . And when you see a canine strange . . . You start another
fight . . . Your tummy nearly scrapes the ground . . . Your ears have
covers floppy . . . But you are neat and clean and sweet . . . And
very seldom sloppy . . . Indeed your only sloppiness . . . Is when you
give a kiss . . . Especially when you lick the hand . . . Of our dear
daughter, Kris.

THIS DAY WITH YOU

I write this letter to your heart . . . In sweet and happy mood . . .
As my own heart is filled with love . . . And lasting gratitude . . .
This day has meant so much to me . . . In all the ways there are . . .
Indeed, just being near you was . . . Like floating on a star . . . You
were so gentle and so kind . . . And trusting in me, too . . . I could
not find the words to say . . . My gratefulness to you . . . And that is
why I take this means . . . Of trying to express . . . My thanks to you,
my darling, for . . . Your loving tenderness . . . And now I write this
postscript—that . . . I hope and wish and pray . . . A very soon tomorrow will . . . Become our wedding day.

TIME TO ENROLL

This time of year is windup time . . . For students on vacation . . . Who are intent on college or . . . High school matriculation . . . It's time to leave the swimming pool . . . And get enrollment ready . . . For any course in which they hope . . . Their progress will be steady . . . It's time to stop their fishing and . . . Their loafing and their dreaming . . . And seriously begin to do . . . Some real scholastic scheming . . . They cannot take their time and wait . . . Until the final minute . . . They must get on their toes right now . . . To put their spirit in it . . . It's time to cut vacations off . . . For those who want more knowledge . . . As they are truly interested . . . In high school or in college.

GOD BLESS OUR 29TH

I thank you, sweetheart, for my joys . . . These nine and twenty years . . . And ask you to forgive me for . . . Your very smallest tears . . . All happiness that I have had . . . Has come to me from you . . . As you have been so good to me . . . So wonderful and true . . . I thank you for our children and . . . Their every quality . . . Which proves how well you've guided and . . . Improved our family . . . God bless you for each sacrifice . . . And all that you have done . . . To help us and inspire us . . . To every victory won . . . And bless you most especially . . . For every weary sigh . . . While staying nine and twenty years . . . With such a guy as I.

DRIVE, STAY ALIVE

If you are on the highway now . . . Please do remember this . . . It is no place to gaze around . . . Or have an extra kiss . . . Please keep your eyes upon the road . . . Your hands upon the wheel . . . And do remember that this life . . . Is very, very real . . . Let not your mind imagine that . . . You merely roll along . . . That driving is a simple thing . . . As easy as a song . . . Remember that the other guy . . . Is dangerous as you . . . Each accident must be the blame . . . Of either one of two . . . And do not ever take a drink . . . Before you start to drive . . . You may become the one who has . . . No chance to stay alive.

IF WORK SEEMS HARD

If work seems hard to tackle when . . . The holidays are gone . . . Be
grateful that you have your health . . . And life is going on . . . That
God allowed your heart to beat . . . Into another year . . . To be
with loving relatives . . . And all your friends so dear . . . Thank Him
for home and hearth and for . . . Your opportunities . . . And for the
inspiration of . . . Your treasured memories . . . Behold the new-
born calendar . . . With holidays in store . . . That may be even
happier . . . Than those you had before . . . So be sincerely grateful
for . . . The task you have to do . . . As it is obvious that God . . . Is
really good to you.

IDLE HANDS

Idle hands are useless hands . . . That turn no spinning wheel . . .
Idle hands are lazy hands . . . That close no business deal . . . They
never seal a friendship or . . . Salute our country's flag . . . They only
stop machinery . . . And make production lag . . . They do not seek
the begger's cup . . . To drop a penny in . . . And they are not the
upraised hands . . . That help some cause to win . . . Idle hands are
foolish hands . . . That never fold in prayer . . . Or try to help the
crippled one . . . With crutches or a chair . . . Their fruitfulness is
always at . . . The very lowest level . . . Except as they are toiling in
. . . The workshop of the devil.

STAGE MANAGER

Stage managers are persons who . . . Are sort of inbetween . . . They
are important to a play . . . But they are never seen . . . Their job is
to make certain that . . . All props are in their place . . . And that
the make-up is correct . . . On every actor's face . . . To check the
scenery and such . . . And to avoid the crime . . . Of actors failing
to appear . . . Upon the stage in time . . . They are the real authority
. . . Behind the curtain drawn . . . Without their watchfulness back-
stage . . . The show could not go on . . . They seldom get the credit
that . . . They actually deserve . . . But they should get a medal for
. . . The silent way they serve.

TIME TO TELL ME

I think that it is time for you . . . To tell me how you feel . . . If you are merely interested . . . Or if your love is real . . . I am a patient person but . . . There has to be an end . . . Are you in love with me, my dear . . . Or are you just a friend? . . . Are you sincere, and possibly . . . Too hesitant and shy . . . Or would it make no difference if . . . Today we said good-by? . . . I cannot wait much longer, so . . . I ask you to declare . . . Your true intention toward my heart . . . And thereby play it fair . . . I cannot wait forever, dear . . . As much as I love you . . . I have to know for certain that . . . You really love me too.

I WON'T FORGET YOU

No, I shall not forget you, friend . . . When I must move away . . . And that is why I leave with you . . . My new address today . . . I'll always want to hear from you . . . By wire, mail or phone . . . As frequently as you have time . . . That you may call your own . . . Still more importantly, I hope . . . That often there will be . . . Surprising opportunities . . . When you may visit me . . . And meanwhile I assure you that . . . Whatever else I do . . . I shall remember you, and I . . . Shall keep in touch with you . . . And anytime that I may have . . . The chance to come back here . . . I hope to prove to you, my friend . . . How much I am sincere.

HAIL OUR FLAG

Display our flag, and raise it high . . . For all the world to see . . . The symbol of our country and . . . Of human liberty . . . Parade our banner on the street . . . With joy and thrilling pride . . . As now we march together and . . . Forever side by side . . . Old Glory with its stars and stripes . . . So beautiful and great . . . A stripe for every colony . . . A star for every state . . . This is the emblem of our land . . . In red and white and blue . . . That guards us, and that summons us . . . When battle we must do . . . Let no one pause or stammer or . . . In any manner lag . . . But all be loyal as we pledge . . . Allegiance to our flag.

BEGGARS ALL

Who is a beggar, after all? . . . The one upon the street . . . Who
holds a cup and does not have . . . The use of hands or feet? . . . Or
is he one who rings the bell . . . Or knocks upon the door . . . To get
a bit of supper and . . . Perhaps a little more? . . . Yes, they are
beggars, all of them . . . But there are others too . . . As much as you
may ask for me . . . And I may pray for you . . . As much as I can
help you now . . . In problems great or small . . . Or as my heart
depends on you . . . Whenever I may call . . . We all are beggars in
a way . . . As humans have to live . . . If only at the throne of God
. . . We beg Him to forgive.

KEEP PRAYING

It matters not how much we ask . . . When any prayer we speak . . .
How many blessings for our friends . . . Or for ourselves we seek . . .
God does not mind how often or . . . How pleadingly we call . . .
Indeed He warmly welcomes our . . . Petitions, one and all . . . But
we must understand that by . . . His wisdom great forever . . . Some
prayers are answered very soon . . . Some later, and some never . . .
For He knows what is best for us . . . And all for whom we pray . . .
And whether He should help us more . . . Than we deserve today
. . . And so each time we beg of God . . . Some favor to fulfill . . .
Let us be patiently resigned . . . To His most holy will.

MERCHANDISING

Merchandising is an art . . . Not just a way to tell . . . About some
articles that you . . . Are hoping you will sell . . . It is that special
manner of . . . Promoting a campaign . . . To show your customers
how much . . . They are so sure to gain . . . The aim of merchandising is . . . To sell not one but two . . . Of any item which they may
. . . Decide to buy from you . . . You must present a program that
. . . Imparts a strong appeal . . . And if you boast a quality . . . Be
sure that it is real . . . Your customers appreciate . . . The bargain
ads they see . . . But they will never tolerate . . . The least dishonesty.

ALL LOVE NOT LOST

When you have loved and you have lost . . . It need not be in vain
. . . A fond and lasting friendship may . . . Turn out to be your gain
. . . There is no reason then to let . . . It get beneath your skin . . .
Or to despise that certain one . . . Whose heart you failed to win . . .
To walk away, and to refuse . . . The very least hello . . . As though
you did not recognize . . . The one you used to know . . . Remember
all the joy you felt . . . When first you fell in love . . . How magic
was the moonlight, and . . . How bright the stars above . . . The love
denied you need not mean . . . A friendship that is dead . . . You
well may be much happier . . . Than if you two had wed.

CIRCUS TIME

Along about this time of year . . . The circus comes to town . . .
With lions and with tigers and . . . The very funny clown . . . With
elephants that usually . . . Begin the big parade . . . While children
munch their popcorn and . . . Consume pink lemonade . . . There
are the bareback riders and . . . The ones who strive to please . . . By
doing stunts upon the ground . . . Or on a high trapeze . . . And
then there are the sideshows, with . . . Their characters so queer . . .
That sometimes make you wonder if . . . Your vision is quite clear
. . . But one thing always certain is . . . That no one wears a frown
. . . When fancy billboards broadcast that . . . The circus is in town.

I LOVE THE SPRING

In many ways I do enjoy . . . The season that is spring . . . But also
there are headaches that . . . This time of year can bring . . . My
wife insists on cleaning house . . . To every nook and corner . . .
And I have not the courage to . . . Defy her or to scorn her . . . Our
home is always spic and span . . . And almost looks like new . . .
But she declares spring-cleaning is . . . The proper thing to do . . .
And so I have to suffer while . . . She satisfies her passion . . . By
renovating everything . . . Because it is the fashion . . . I love the
season that is spring . . . Though it would be more gay . . . If only I
could pack my bags . . . And hie myself away.

HE ONLY GOSSIPS

Why does some person tell the wrongs . . . That other people do . . .
And spread the story far and wide . . . However false or true? . . .
Why does he do it even when . . . The facts are really there . . .
Though no one asks to hear the tale . . . Of how or when or where?
. . . Not anything important, as . . . The nation is concerned . . .
But some small incident he saw . . . Or in some way he learned . . .
Why must his wagging tongue repeat . . . That story all around? . . .
Why is he so insistent on . . . The views he would expound? . . . The
only recognition he . . . Can ever really gain . . . Is that of one more
gossiper . . . Unkind, uncouth and vain.

MAKE SOMEONE GLAD

When you make others glad in life . . . You make God happy too
. . . And for that goodness of your soul . . . He will remember you
. . . Each kindly act, each sacrifice . . . He will reward you for . . .
And he will be your guardian . . . And friend forevermore . . . Be-
cause when you show kindness to . . . Your neighbor on this sod . . .
You do as much in every way . . . To serve almighty God . . . So
spread a little happiness . . . Along your passing scene . . . And do
it frequently enough . . . Until it is routine . . . Make someone glad
he is alive . . . By something that you do . . . And God will give
His blessing great . . . A thousand times to you.

MY BROTHERLY SON

It was a great occasion, and . . . It gave much joy to me . . . When
Don obtained his membership . . . In my fraternity . . . Especially
delightful was . . . My privilege to be there . . . To help initiate my
boy . . . With due fraternal care . . . And so in that respect my son
. . . Became my brother too . . . Entitled to participate . . . In all the
things we do . . . And no one understood so well . . . What it was
all about . . . As my new brother did that day . . . And so I soon
found out . . . With youthful confidence that was . . . Perhaps a
little brash . . . He said to me, "My brother, will . . . You let me have
some cash?"

BE ONE WITH ME

Please do not hide from me, my love . . . Please do not run away . . .
But let me know if anything . . . Disturbs you night or day . . . I
yearn so much to comfort you . . . Should anything go wrong . . .
Because I want your life to be . . . The very sweetest song . . . I
cannot stand the smallest tear . . . Or sad look on your face . . . The
slightest doubt or fear you have . . . I hunger to erase . . . Please
put your confidence in me . . . Let me take care of you . . . Join
hands with me, my dearest one . . . To see all struggles through . . .
And, darling, join your heart with mine . . . For all the years in store
. . . So wonderfully, perfectly . . . In love forevermore.

THE HILLS OF HOPE

The hills of San Francisco are . . . The steps that lead the way . . .
From daily cares to restful thoughts . . . By gazing on the bay . . .
They are the invitation to . . . A quietude of soul . . . For everyone
who ventures there . . . Whatever be his goal . . . The visitor, the
native, and . . . The proud adopted son . . . The happy and successful, and . . . The poor and lonely one . . . Whatever sky or season or . . . The time of day or night . . . The hills of San Francisco
give . . . Each hope a greater height . . . For there is inspiration in
. . . The beauty far and near . . . And life begins all over in . . . That
healthy atmosphere.

MY HUMBLE FRIENDS

My friendships are a thousand now . . . And maybe many more . . .
There are so many souls I meet . . . I cannot keep the score . . . Each
one becomes a kinship as . . . Each face is one more friend . . . And
we are all God's children from . . . Beginning to the end . . . I do not
measure friendship by . . . Success or charming look . . . By public
fame or by the size . . . Of any pocketbook . . . I weigh their value
on the scales . . . Of what they mean to me . . . As much as they extend their hands . . . In all sincerity . . . My friends are those who
humbly live . . . Their lives upon this sod . . . Whose only real im-
portance is . . . Their loyalty to God.

I TOLD YOU SO

Some most unnecessary words . . . Wherever you may go . . . Are
those when someone says to you . . . "You see?—I told you so." . . .
Yes, their prediction was correct . . . But they are most unkind . . .
When they appear to sneer, as they . . . Remember and remind . . .
It is the haughty attitude . . . And quite contemptuous too . . . Of
those who have no right to feel . . . Superior to you . . . Some day
they also may be wrong . . . And very much regret . . . The words of
criticism that . . . They hope you will forget . . . Mistakes are made
by everyone . . . As people live and grow . . . And it is cruel to declare . . . "You see?—I told you so."

GOD, GIVE US REASON

Help us, O God, to follow You . . . In every way we know . . . But
let us not be narrow in . . . The judgment we bestow . . . In telling
others how to live . . . And what they ought to do . . . As all the
world should strive to be . . . A little more like You . . . Indeed we
have no right to judge . . . And often we are blind . . . Whereas You
want our hearts to be . . . Most tolerant and kind . . . Help us, O
God, to keep our faith . . . Yet not to interfere . . . With those who
may think otherwise. . . And may be quite sincere . . . Help us to
mind our own affairs . . . And not be tempted now . . . To take that
narrow attitude . . . Of "holier than thou."

GIVE ME THE KITCHEN

I much prefer the kitchen to . . . A dining room real neat . . .
Somehow a meal of any kind . . . Seems so much more a treat . . .
The breakfast, lunch and dinner and . . . The little bites between
. . . Are tastier and cozier . . . Upon the kitchen scene . . . Of
course a formal banquet in . . . The dining room is fine . . . If you
send invitations for . . . Celebrities to dine . . . But even they, I
think, would feel . . . More comfortable and gay . . . If they could
sit on kitchen stools . . . And eat in their own way . . . And in the
last analysis . . . Considering all the facts . . . Where else but in the
kitchen can . . . You get those midnight snacks?

BE TRUE TO ME

Darling, I depend on you . . . Each moment of each day . . . To comfort and encourage me . . . And keep my tears away . . . Life would be so meaningless . . . Without your loving heart . . . And I would be so miserable . . . If ever we should part . . . You mean everything to me . . . The earth and all the sky . . . The dreams that build tomorrows, and . . . The breath of every sigh . . . Darling, I depend on you . . . For all my energy . . . Life would be an empty glass . . . Without your loyalty . . . Please, be always true to me . . . And never let me go . . . Darling, I depend on you . . . Because I love you so.

OLD HAL

Old Hal has won his laurels as . . . An artist for the press . . . And as a painter who has gained . . . No very small success . . . His history is fabulous . . . A most entrancing story . . . And I would like to tell it, but . . . He does not care for glory . . . However, I can say this much . . . The more important part . . . That all who ever meet him are . . . Forever in his heart . . . He struggles with his soul and brush . . . In every way to serve them . . . He wants to claim them as his friends . . . And thoroughly deserve them . . . But it is they, like you and I . . . Who long to be his pal . . . And are forever grateful for . . . The friendship of Old Hal.

TIME FOR SCHOOL

School is starting up again . . . Which is not bad or sad . . . Vacation-weary boys and girls . . . Are actually quite glad . . . They may not say it right out loud . . . But they are really gay . . . To be with all those friends again . . . In study and in play . . . The summertime is wonderful . . . As happy as can be . . . But finally those careless days . . . Become monotony . . . And then their little hearts rejoice . . . To hear the schoolbell ring . . . And be back in that building, to . . . Take part in everything . . . And though they never would admit . . . That such a thing is true . . . Deep down inside, in every way . . . They love their teachers too.

NO SOUR FACE

However bitter you may feel . . . When you have lost some race . . .
Be not so weak or foolish as . . . To show a sour face . . . Bow not
your head, and do not let . . . Your eyes deplore defeat . . . But show
the courage you will have . . . The next time that you meet . . .
What good can your resentment do . . . When you have lost the
game . . . However much you think that yours . . . Should be the
victor's name? . . . Remember that the judges are . . . As eager to be
fair . . . As you are anxious to become . . . The champion everywhere . . . Give not the smallest angry look . . . Or show a sour face
. . . But prove that you can take defeat . . . With courage and with
grace.

GOD, HELP ME AGAIN

You made me, God—You gave me life . . . And I belong to You . . .
And I should be obedient . . . In everything I do . . . Obedient to
all Your laws . . . And grateful for Your grace . . . And for my daily
strength to meet . . . The trials I must face . . . I do acknowledge
You, My God . . . I worship on my knees . . . I am Your own with
heart and soul . . . My mind and memories . . . I know all this, my
God, and yet . . . How sorry is my plight . . . Because so often what
I do . . . Is wrong instead of right . . . Forgive me for my failures,
God . . . And help me start anew . . . The kind of life on earth You
want . . . To have me live for You.

WE NEED OUR DIGITS

My dear wife smashed her finger as . . . She slammed our auto's door
. . . And now that finger wears a cast . . . And it is very sore . . . A
letter from a friend revealed . . . A somewhat ailing toe . . . That
caused not just annoyance but . . . Much misery and woe . . . Such
hurts are not uncommon, yet . . . They show how little we . . .
Appreciate our digits all . . . Until some injury . . . Our fingers are
important as . . . We work and eat and write . . . And we need toes
to dance or walk . . . A rope or wire tight . . . So let us be real careful
of . . . Our digits every day . . . And guard them as we use them in
. . . Each tough or gentle way.

EACH TIME I GAZE

Each time I see a flower shop . . . With flowers pink and blue . . . I think of babies beautiful . . . And someone sweet as you . . . I dream of something possible . . . If you were mine to hold . . . But you are far beyond my reach . . . Of silver or of gold . . . Of course, I have not asked you, and . . . I may be very wrong . . . Perhaps you would accept my heart . . . And make my life a song . . . But I have not the courage now . . . For such a bold approach . . . Indeed the subject is not one . . . That I would ever broach . . . But, oh, I wish it could be so . . . For as I gaze at you . . . I know that only your sweet self . . . Could make my dream come true.

CROSS-COUNTRY

Cross-country is America . . . Of least applauded names . . . As life goes on from day to day . . . With labor or with games . . . Cross-country is a proving ground . . . For those who like to race . . . As college varsities compete . . . To win the highest place . . . It is the area in which . . . Fresh crops become a load . . . For farmers' trucks to haul along . . . The farm-to-market road . . . Where barefoot boys go fishing with . . . A plain old bamboo pole . . . Or dive into the water of . . . A hidden swimming hole . . . Cross-country is America . . . Beyond the cities tall . . . Where women cook, and chickens scratch . . . And leaves and snowflakes fall.

OUT-OF-TOWN FRIENDS

We like to entertain our friends . . . Wherever they may live . . . With all the hospitality . . . And comfort we can give . . . The poor as we, the average . . . And those who gain renown . . . But most especially the ones . . . Who come from out of town . . . Because we seldom see them, and . . . As they decide to roam . . . It really brings us happiness . . . To make them feel at home . . . We entertain our local friends . . . As much, from day to day . . . As we can fill their hearts with joy . . . And bless them on their way . . . But as for those from out of town . . . The ones we seldom see . . . We go all-out, although we may . . . Be broke as we can be.

I HAVE TO ENVY

I walk along the sidewalk and . . . I watch the cars go by . . . And
now and then I do indulge . . . In just a little sigh . . . Sometimes I
wish I could afford . . . That kind of luxury . . . Especially the mod-
els new . . . In motor industry . . . And then I think of other costs
. . . Those drivers have to pay . . . Including house and taxes and
. . . Their groceries every day . . . Their worries seem to multiply
. . . The more they try to earn . . . And I remember I am free . . .
Of worry and concern . . . And yet I have to envy them . . . As now
their cars go by . . . Because they obviously are quite . . . More com-
petent than I.

GOD HELPS THOSE—

I pray to God for everything . . . I need upon my shelf . . . Except
His help in any way . . . That I can help myself . . . Because I
know His charity . . . And all that He will do . . . To lift me in
my sorrow and . . . To see my struggle through . . . God loves me
and He guides me to . . . The corners of the earth . . . But also
He expects of me . . . To prove my lasting worth . . . He wants me
to adore Him and . . . Obey His each command . . . And as I
strive to serve Him, He . . . Will lead me by the hand . . . But if
I do not help myself . . . To do God's holy will . . . There is no
prayer that I can hope . . . He ever will fulfill.

YOUR FLAG DAY

I love our flag, the stars and stripes . . . The red, the white, the blue
. . . And every time I see it, dear . . . My thoughts are turned to
you . . . Because your words inspired me . . . To don a uniform
. . . And be prepared to guard our land . . . Against whatever
storm . . . Yes, I am patriotic, and . . . I want to do my part . . .
But it is so much easier . . . With courage from your heart . . . You
know that I am willing, dear . . . To pay the highest price . . . The
same as you resign yourself . . . To every sacrifice . . . And yet I must
salute you on . . . This Flag Day meant for you . . . As you are helping me to serve . . . With faith and courage true.

MY ONLY ONE FOREVER

You are not the only one . . . My heart has ever known . . . Yours
are not the only lips . . . That ever kissed my own . . . Yours
are not the only eyes . . . That whispered tenderly . . . And yours
are not the only arms . . . That held me lovingly . . . But no one
else in all my life . . . Has ever meant so much . . . And no one
else could ever have . . . Your soft, endearing touch . . . No one
else could ever match . . . The magic in your eyes . . . Your character and all the ways . . . In which you are so wise . . . The others
are forgotten, and . . . Without the least regret . . . I only wish that
you had been . . . The first I ever met.

OLD SHOES

Old shoes reveal the story of . . . A man who walks the street . . .
In search of some employment or . . . To beg a bite to eat . . .
They are the footwear of the waif . . . That poor, neglected lad . . .
Whose life is lonely but who is . . . Too busy to be sad . . . Or
maybe they belong to her . . . Who scrubs the floors at night . . .
To help her kids or husband through . . . A budget worse than
tight . . . Old shoes enclose the tired feet . . . Of office workers
too . . . Whose pay is insufficient for . . . Their wives and babies
new . . . They are the kind of worn-out shoes . . . With bottoms
that are holes . . . And as those people wear them, may . . . God
bless their humble souls.

HE HOPED FOR PEACE

If Lincoln were our president . . . In this new age and day . . . I
wonder what dear Abraham . . . Would be inclined to say . . . I
think that tears would fill his eyes . . . For he would be so sad . . .
To see the turmoil of a few . . . That makes all people mad . . . I
think when his decree went forth . . . He meant it not to be . . .
For every issue to be solved . . . So swiftly, suddenly . . . He must
have prayed for tolerance . . . And patience on each side . . . To
sensibly deliberate . . . And take each step in stride . . . If he had
known what was to come . . . It would have grieved his heart . . .
That victory could only mean . . . Another war would start.

I HAVE NO FEAR

I do not fear the hopes and dreams . . . That science my fulfill
. . . For I believe all things must be . . . According to God's will
If now atomic energy . . . And search in outer space . . . Made
possible the whole wide world . . . To suddenly erase . . . I still
would not have any fear . . . Of total tragedy . . . For it could happen only as . . . God wanted it to be . . . If He commanded peace
on earth . . . No one could interfere . . . Except as man defied
Him, with . . . The punishment quite clear . . . And even then man
could not rule . . . The wondrous earth we know . . . For everything alive must be . . . The way God wants it so.

NOT PRAYER ALONE

We cannot get to heaven by . . . The simple means of prayer . . .
We have to earn God's great reward . . . By doing our full share . . .
By treating everyone we meet . . . With love and charity . . . And
even treating strangers in . . . A manner neighborly . . . A prayer
is just a plea for help . . . That earns no special credit . . . And it
is not sufficient to . . . Eliminate a debit . . . Unless it is a prayer
of thanks . . . For favors far or near . . . That really heartfelt sentiment . . . God always likes to hear . . . But prayers for help and
guiding grace . . . Though always good to say . . . Cannot ensure
salvation for . . . Our soul in any way.

BOOKBINDER

Bookbinding is the ancient art . . . That folds and sews and trims
. . . The pages filled with diverse prose . . . Or poetry or hymns
. . . And fastens them securely to . . . The cover that is there . . .
To help preserve the published tome . . . From daily wear and tear
. . . No book can be complete without . . . The good bookbinder's
knack . . . Of giving his own special touch . . . To both the front
and back . . . However skilled the author is . . . His volume still
depends . . . Upon the expert workmanship . . . That someone else
extends . . . The publisher may love it, and . . . It may win wide
appeal . . . But that bookbinder is the one . . . Who must sew up
the deal.

BEAUTY AND LIGHT

Beauty and light go hand in hand . . . Because there cannot be
. . . Real beauty in the dark of night . . . For human eyes to see
. . . There is no color in the dark . . . That ever can be seen . . . The
yellow, orange, violet . . . The blue, the red or green . . . And so the
beauty of our lives . . . As we pursue our way . . . Depends upon our
virtues, as . . . We spend each passing day . . . If we are kind to
others, then . . . Our star will shine real bright . . . And always it will
penetrate . . . The darkness of the night . . . For as the soul is beautiful . . . It gives illumination . . . And light and beauty surely are
. . . The perfect combination.

I NEED JUST FAITH

I need not eyes to see . . . Nor ears to hear . . . If by my faith in
God . . . I have no fear . . . I need no hand to touch . . . No feet
to stand . . . As long as I obey . . . His each command . . . No lung
or nose to breathe . . . The fragrant air . . . No lips with which to
smile . . . Or kisses share . . . Not even sympathy . . . To carry on
. . . With sunshine promising . . . A brighter dawn . . . If now my
body fails . . . To make the grade . . . There is no reason I . . .
Should be afraid . . . I need just faith in God . . . With heart and
soul . . . As He has said my faith . . . Will make me whole.

TRUE FAMILY

How many of us understand . . . What makes a family? . . . it is not
just a man and wife . . . And children two or three . . . They all may
live together, and . . . They may have prominence . . . And yet not
be a family . . . In that most special sense . . . Because no family
exists . . . As something whole and true . . . Unless each member
really joins . . . In what the others do . . . Unless they share each
other's joy . . . And sacrifice and love . . . And pray together for the
help . . . They need from God above . . . A family is not composed
. . . Of just the persons in it . . . But also their united goal . . .
And how they work to win it.

TO LOVE AGAIN

Unfortunately someone wrote . . . What we so well recall . . . "It's
better to have loved and lost . . . Than never loved at all" . . .
Because some lovers love this thought . . . While their affinity . . .
Is not for someone else but for . . . Dramatic tragedy . . . They
dream of recognition for . . . The "suffering" they bear . . .
And swear there's no one else for whom . . . They'd ever come to
care . . . Oh, yes, a love affair can be . . . A somewhat tragic thing
. . . And sometimes it can really leave . . . A deep and painful
sting . . . But feeling sorry for ourselves . . . Is not the answer
then . . . The world is filled with lovers and . . . With time to love
again.

RED CLIFFS

The Red Cliffs of New Mexico . . . Originally were gray . . .
Until a great stag, wounded, left . . . His blood along the way . . .
And so the rocks and hills turned red . . . And some of them quite
black . . . While rain poured down occasionally . . . To cover every
track . . . It is an ancient legend that . . . The Navajos repeat . . .
Some demon was the cause of it . . . For victory complete . . . The
demon wanted to destroy . . . All of New Mexico . . . To under-
mine the people and . . . Make his empire grow . . . But now the
Red Cliffs reach so high . . . And so majestically . . . They seem
to lift our hearts to God . . . And to eternity.

HELLO? YES. HI!

I like to tease Kristina dear . . . About the telephone . . . The
way she always answers it . . . With certain words and tone . . . I
mean, each time the call is from . . . Some special girl or boy . . .
Whose thoughtfulness in phoning fills . . . Her youthful heart with
joy . . . She says "Hello?" then "Yes," then "Hi!" . . . Her every-
day routine . . . And I am sure I understand . . . What those ex-
pressions mean . . . The "yes" conveys, "Yes, this is Kris" . . . And
then when they reply . . . And tell her who is calling, she . . .
Excitedly says "Hi!" . . . Dear daughter did not realize this . . .
Until I made it known . . . Now we both laugh each time when
she . . . Lifts up the telephone.

HOW OLD ARE YOU?

How old are you according to . . . The record of your birth? . . .
And then again how old are you . . . According to your worth? . . .
Sometimes your age is measured by . . . Your actual birthday date
. . . If only by the government . . . To keep the record straight
. . . But in the more important sense . . . Your years are young or
old . . . As you give up too easily . . . Or you are brave and bold
. . . And if the problems you have faced . . . And trials you've
endured . . . Have shaped the true integrity . . . Which proves you
have matured . . . The only age that really counts . . . Is that of
being wise . . . With prudence and humility . . . To help you
grow in size.

O MOTHER DEAR!

O Mother dear, I love you so! . . . How wonderful you are! . . .
Just like a guardian angel and . . . My ever guiding star . . . I
love you for your gentle care . . . And understanding mind . . .
And for the million ways in which . . . Your heart has been so
kind . . . For every sacrifice and all . . . The time and energy . . .
To give me comfort, and to bring . . . More happiness to me . . .
I could not ever pay you back . . . And you would want no pay
. . . But I do promise, Mother dear . . . To live your words each
day . . . And on this very special day . . . For mothers everywhere
. . . May God be extra good to you . . . In answer to my prayer.

THINK AND DO

There is an early grade school book . . . Entitled, "Think and Do"
. . . That tells no grown-up anything . . . That is exactly new . . .
But we could learn a lesson from . . . The title of that book . . .
If we would take the patience and . . . A little time to look . . .
How often do we stop and think? . . . What deeds are ours to boast?
. . . How frequently do we relax . . . And simply sit and coast? . . .
We do not use our brains enough . . . We do not try our best . . .
To climb the heights that challenge us . . . Until we reach the
crest . . . We ought to turn our lazy eyes . . . To seek horizons new
. . . And use our stamina and brains . . . To really think and do.

HAVE I TOLD YOU?

Have I told you lately, dear . . . How much you mean to me . . .
With your smile of comfort and . . . Your constant sympathy? With
your understanding heart . . . When I have lost a fight? . . . Proud
of me for doing what . . . I really thought was right? . . . Have I told
you lately, dear . . . The thanks I should express . . . For all the
countless ways in which . . . You bring me happiness? . . . Have I
whispered lately, dear . . . As often I should do . . . "Forgive me for
the troubles I . . . Am always causing you?" . . . No, I guess not
lately, dear . . . Have I fulfilled my part . . . But, darling, all these
sentiments . . . Are always in my heart.

DREAMER

A dreamer is a person who . . . Is wishing in his mind . . . For
some success or happiness . . . That he would like to find . . . He
may be one who dissipates . . . The hours of the day . . . In visions
made of vapor that . . . The wind will blow away . . . Or he may
be the one whose dreams . . . Reflect intense ambition . . . To serve
him as a stimulant . . . In seeking recognition . . . There is the
wealthy dreamer who . . . Has nothing else to do . . . And who is
merely passing time . . . In search of something new . . . And then
there is the one who floats . . . On fleecy clouds above . . . Who
cannot help his wishful dreams . . . Because he is in love.

NIGHT FOR FRIENDS

One night is worth a thousand days . . . No matter what the
weather . . . If that is when new friends are made . . . As people
get together . . . Not temporary friends but those . . . Who stay
forever true . . . And with their kindness and their love . . . Mean
everything to you . . . It does not happen often but . . . There are
those warm embraces . . . When you become enchanted by . . .
Their really friendly faces . . . And very likely they are those . . .
Who last throughout the years . . . Forever here and everywhere . . .
To share your smiles and tears . . . Friends are made both day and
night . . . But usually at nighttime . . . Somehow in social gather-
ings . . . It seems to be the right time.

HOW SAY WE?

One day by some acquaintance I . . . Was asked quite suddenly
. . . To say in just a few small words . . . My whole philosophy
. . . It was a mental challenge and . . . It took me by surprise . . .
I floundered hopelessly, and yet . . . It opened up my eyes . . . How
many of us stop to think . . . About the way we feel . . . Re-
garding life from day to day . . . And what is false or real? . . .
How many of us could express . . . The dreams that are our goal
. . . In just a simple phrase or two . . . That would reveal our
soul? . . . And if we told the truth, could we . . . Possess a conscience clear? . . . Do we pursue the best ideals . . . In every way
sincere?

GOD IS OBVIOUS

God is so obvious to us . . . How can we ever doubt . . . As we
consider sun and moon . . . And all the stars about? . . . As we
consider life itself . . . The river, tree and field . . . The wind and
rain, the warmth and cold . . . And all the crops they yield . . .
And then there is the human side . . . The baby in its crib . . . And
all the Homo Sapiens . . . That came from Adam's rib . . . The man
or woman of today . . . Who hears and speaks and sees . . . A creature
that is free on earth . . . To do as it may please . . . How else can
anyone explain . . . Our source upon this sod . . . Except, as it is
obvious . . . Our one, almighty God.

INTERRUPTION

An interruption in our work . . . Becomes a time for play . . .
And that is good, as it may help . . . Relax us on our way . . . A
coffee-break or any kind . . . Of rest that we may get . . . But not
if it is so prolonged . . . That it may cause regret . . . Sometimes
an interruption can . . . Obstruct our working view . . . And we
are tempted to neglect . . . The things we ought to do . . . Our
time should be apportioned so . . . Important work is done . . .
With reasonable allowance for . . . A share of rest and fun . . . An
interruption can be good . . . Or it can go too far . . . Depending
on its use and how . . . Intelligent we are.

SNOW IN JANUARY

Snow in January . . . Is never a surprise . . . But many times it does become . . . A blessing in disguise . . . It may produce pneumonia or . . . A cold or rasping cough . . . Or some discomfort of a kind . . . You cannot just laugh off . . . But snow in January can . . . Be quite a benefit . . . For those who may be well prepared . . . To be enjoying it . . . Snow in January brings . . . That moisture to the field . . . Which helps the farmer's winter wheat . . . Become a greater yield . . . It helps the sled and ski and all . . . Who love that winter scene . . . Of earth adorned in white before . . . It turns again to green.

MY SILENT MESSAGE

If you could hear the words I say . . . When I am all alone . . . I would not have to tell you, dear . . . I want you for my own . . . Because when I am by myself . . . Or walking in a crowd . . . Where I am sure I am not heard . . . I say those words out loud . . . But when I see you face to face . . . I cannot be so bold . . . And so my lips are silent and . . . My message is untold . . . I simply am too bashful to . . . Declare my love to you . . . And everything you mean to me . . . In all I think and do . . . And so I write this letter as . . . My only way to try . . . And fondly hope that you will send . . . A favorable reply.

BEAUTIFUL CITY

There is a growing movement now . . . To make surroundings gay . . . In town or city where we live . . . Or where we work each day . . . To beautify the downtown streets . . . And every neighborhood . . . And fashion that appearance which . . . Is clean and bright and good . . . And that is worthy in itself . . . And wonderful indeed . . . Provided, first of all, that we . . . Take care of those in need . . . Replacing slums with housing that . . . Will make it fit to live . . . And furnishing all services . . . We are obliged to give . . . To smooth out traffic, and provide . . . Protection everywhere . . . These are much prettier because . . . They prove how much we care.

GOOD LUCK, KRIS

Next month our darling daughter will . . . Start in a private school . . . To conquer some more inches on . . . Her long scholastic rule . . . These are the senior high school years . . . A little hard to take . . . But I am confident about . . . The marks that she will make . . . Because she has a brilliant mind . . . As all the records show . . . And being like her mother dear . . . Most anyone should know . . . That she will be a credit to . . . The school in every way . . . And as the years go by, they will . . . Be proud of her some day . . . Good luck, Kristina darling, and . . . God bless you night and dawn . . . With all the courage and the faith . . . To help you carry on.

HOW TRUE ARE YOU?

Do you remember when we met . . . And when I said to you . . . That you were gentle as the rain . . . And soft as skies of blue? . . . Do you recall that darkness and . . . The very time and place . . . When I embraced and kissed you and . . . You quickly slapped my face? . . . My cheek was really stinging but . . . The feeling was so sweet . . . I knew there would be other times . . . When you and I would meet . . . And then your heart relented and . . . You let me call on you . . . With every opportunity . . . To prove I would be true . . . Do you remember all those days . . . As I have kept my vow . . . And can you tell me, dearest, you . . . Are just as faithful now?

STORM SIGNALS

Storm signals are the flags that fly . . . With black on field of red . . . Or lights at night, of red or white . . . For danger dead ahead . . . They are the warning semaphores . . . The lightship bells that ring . . . Below the water, when the fog . . . Is shrouding everything . . . So, too, there are the signals in . . . Our life from day to day . . . To warn us of a human storm . . . That may be on its way . . . The flicker of an eyelash or . . . The squeezing of a hand . . . To guard against an argument . . . And help us understand . . . Whatever warning, let us heed . . . And be prepared to meet . . . The danger that could otherwise . . . Accomplish our defeat.

NO FINER FRIEND

Sometimes a dullness clouds your mind . . . And sort of shrouds your view . . . And then someone approaches and . . . Brings confidence to you . . . Someone who pats you on the back . . . For something you have done . . . And honestly believes in you . . . In battles to be won . . . Who lifts you from your lethargy . . . Or maybe your despair . . . And who revives your courage and . . . Your readiness to dare . . . Well, if and when that happens, you . . . May write it in your book . . . There is no greater friend on earth . . . No matter where you look . . . There is no finer person than . . . The one who takes your hand . . . And leads you to the peaceful place . . . Where people understand.

HOW MANY FAVORS?

How many favors have you done . . . Throughout the passing years? . . . How often have you taken time . . . To calm somebody's fears? . . . What seconds have you tried to spare . . . From any night or day . . . To do the kindly deed that helps . . . Someone along his way? . . . You need not be a millionaire . . . With cash to spare and spend . . . The only thing you have to do . . . Is just to be a friend . . . To give an introduction or . . . Help clear a worthy name . . . By telling what you know to free . . . Some suspect from the blame . . . How many favors have you done . . . Or have you tried to do? . . . Those little inconveniences . . . That should not bother you?

I NEED YOU, GOD

I need You, God, each day of life . . . I need You everywhere . . . When I am filled with joy, and when . . . My heart is in despair . . . I need You when I have success . . . To keep reminding me . . . The only glory worth my while . . . Is in eternity . . . I need You when I falter and . . . I fall along the way . . . When I am miserable, dear God . . . And all the skies are gray . . . For only You can save me when . . . I am about to sink . . . And only You can help my mind . . . The way it ought to think . . . I need You, God—please give me all . . . The grace and strength to win . . . Your blessing for each effort and . . . Forgiveness for each sin.

OUR GREAT AMERICA

What is America today? . . . A nation great and strong? . . . Yes,
it is that but so much more . . . It is a wondrous song . . . A song
of happiness and love . . . And children's laughter loud . . . And
all the worthwhile things that would . . . Make anybody proud . . .
It is the land of freedom for . . . All citizens to share . . . With
equal opportunities . . . And safeguards everywhere . . . It is the
country schoolhouse and . . . The happy, peaceful farm . . . And
brotherly protection when . . . There is the least alarm . . . America
is freedom true . . . In thought and word and deed . . . With loving
care for anyone . . . Who is in desperate need.

FOR REAL, FOREVER

I loved you, dear, completely from . . . The moment that we met
. . . Because the way you gazed at me . . . I never could forget
. . . Perhaps you did not really mean . . . That lovelight in your
eyes . . . And maybe I mistakingly . . . Interpreted your sighs . . .
But, oh, you gave my heart the hope . . . It never had before . . . And
I am waiting patiently . . . To knock upon your door . . . Please let
me know sincerely now . . . The way you truly feel . . . And whether
your affection, dear . . . Is really, really real . . . Please tell me that
you love me, and . . . Your love is ever true . . . And with my heart
for evermore . . . I will belong to you.

SPORTSMANSHIP

Sportsmanship is something that . . . You cannot steal or buy . . .
Because it is the product of . . . How hard you really try . . . It is
the spirit of the heart . . . You put into a game . . . To play it fair,
without regard . . . For any claim to fame . . . It is the emblem
of your soul . . . As you are real sincere . . . In striving to be worthy
of . . . Each handshake and each cheer . . . And more importantly
the strength . . . To take it standing up . . . When you feel sure
you should have won . . . A medal or a cup . . . Sportsmanship is
honest play . . . And taking things in stride . . . As you perform
your best, so God . . . Is always at your side.

HER DAY WITH DADDY

Each Saturday Kristina sings . . . And goes to drama class . . .
And equally my leisure time . . . I have to overpass . . . Because I
have to take her to . . . Her lessons on that day . . . And Saturday
belongs to her . . . In every other way . . . It is her day with Daddy
that . . . Belongs to us alone . . . With lunch in some secluded
place . . . And shopping on her own . . . She loves to go from
store to store . . . And see the sights in town . . . And whether
there is sun or rain . . . She never wears a frown . . . It is a bit ex-
pensive, but . . . I love to hear her say . . . "I thank you, Daddy
dearest, for . . . A happy Saturday."

OUR WILL TO LIVE

What is this thing called "courage?" . . . How can it be defined?
. . . And when and how in life can it . . . Be really underlined?
. . . Well, physically, of course, it is . . . That certain bravery . . .
Which risks the body and the heart . . . For all humanity . . . A
crushing blow to any town . . . In time of peace or war . . . Inspires
every human heart . . . To do a little more . . . But it takes mental
courage to . . . Exist from day to day . . . And that is what we need
the most . . . As we pursue our way . . . Courage is our will to live
. . . A single minute longer . . . And with each minute of that
kind . . . We grow a little stronger.

THIS YEAR WE PRAY

This Sunday, by the grace of God . . . We start another year . . .
We hope the weather will be calm . . . And all the heavens clear
. . . We pray for peace and happiness . . . And progress on this
earth . . . With opportunity to prove . . . Our individual worth
. . . May there be fewer tragedies . . . A smaller traffic toll . . .
And captured every criminal . . . Who sells his wicked soul . . .
May there be love and brotherhood . . . And boundless charity . . .
For all the peoples of the world . . . And every family . . . We pray to
God for food and drink . . . For guidance and for grace . . . And for
salvation in the end . . . For all the human race.

KENNEL PALS

We took our dachshund, Pretzel, to . . . The kennel for a stay . . .
Because we had to travel and . . . He would be in our way . . . Of
course he missed us terribly . . . As he has done before . . . Each
time he could not be with us . . . Upon the bed or floor . . . And
yet he seemed quite eager to . . . Pick up his reservation . . . As
he was met by curious stares . . . Or barks of real elation . . . It
seemed as though the other dogs . . . Gave love and sympathy . . .
To one more member of their kind . . . In close captivity . . . He
probably was happy with . . . Those canine guys and gals . . . But
now back home he never whines . . . To see his kennel pals.

YOUR GOLDEN DAY

God grant you every blessing on . . . Your Golden Wedding Day
. . . You both deserve the highest praise . . . Along your happy way
. . . Fifty years together now . . . Still walking arm in arm . . .
Sharing all your smiles and tears . . . Life with all its charm . . .
Together in your dreams come true . . . Beyond the seven seas
. . . With kisses and embraces and . . . The sweetest memories
. . . Memories of long ago . . . When first you met and blushed
. . . While all the world became your own . . . And every sound
was hushed . . . May this your anniversary . . . Be really filled with
gold . . . As much as all the happiness . . . The human heart can
hold.

WAS IT A DREAM?

Last night, while wandering in the park . . . I saw you standing
there . . . With starlight in your wistful eyes . . . And moonbeams
on your hair . . . I thought I heard you whisper that . . . You still
belonged to me . . . Beyond the vale of shadows and . . . All
forms of fantasy . . . And then the vision disappeared . . . Your
smiling face was gone . . . And I went home to sleep until . . .
Another lonely dawn . . . You looked so real last night, my love
. . . But now it surely seems . . . That it was just another of . . .
My many wishful dreams . . . And yet I do remember I . . . Was
in the park last night . . . And any test will prove I still . . . Have
20-20 sight.

COWBOY BOOTS

Cowboy boots are beautiful . . . And practical to wear . . . But
making them requires tools . . . And certain skill and care . . .
The "crimping" and the "lasting" and . . . The molding of the
sole . . . And every process that presents . . . Its own important
role . . . "Inseeming" boots and staining them . . . And heeling
them just right . . . And adding on the stitching that . . . Is fanci-
ful and bright . . . Two hundred operations must . . . Be carried
out before . . . We see those stylish cowboy boots . . . Displayed
in any store . . . Cowboy boots can do so much . . . To boost
their owner's pride . . . But few, if any, feet know why . . . They
feel so good inside.

NOT JUST HELLO

Life can be so beautiful . . . And it can be so sweet . . . If only
we are interested . . . In people whom we meet . . . If only we
extend our thoughts . . . Beyond a mere hello . . . And strive a
bit unselfishly . . . To help a friendship grow . . . Just to linger
there a while . . . And be most gracious then . . . And set a certain time and place . . . Where we shall meet again . . . "Hello"
is such a happy word . . . And yet so very small . . . That it can
vanish swiftly from . . . The moments we recall . . . So let us try
to cultivate . . . Each person whom we meet . . . Our dearest
friend may be the one . . . We incidentally meet.

NO SINGLE DAY

No hopes and dreams depend upon . . . A single day of life . . .
There is no sudden victory . . . To overcome all strife . . . Life
is a process that goes on . . . From one day to the next . . . However happy we may be . . . Or dubious or vexed . . . We must be
patient as we think . . . And in the way we talk . . . There will be
time enough to run . . . When we have learned to walk . . . So
let us take it easy as . . . We want to win our way . . . And not
attempt another Rome . . . In just a single day . . . A miracle or
tragedy . . . Could happen overnight . . . But normally all life on
earth . . . Is just a common plight.

HELP ME GUIDE THEM

Dear God, please bless my children, and . . . Protect them every day . . . And help me guide and counsel them . . . As they go on their way . . . Enable me to answer well . . . The questions that they ask . . . And be of some assistance when . . . They face a strenuous task . . . To teach them every right from wrong . . . And how to play the game . . . In order to achieve and to . . . Preserve a worthy name . . . And more than any other thing . . . Please help me, God, to be . . . A really good example for . . . My loving family . . . Help me to hide my own mistakes . . . So they will never know . . . While they would imitate my life . . . As mentally they grow.

THEY'LL STAY IN LOVE

Classes now are at an end . . . For this scholastic year . . . And you can hear the pupils and . . . The tired teachers cheer . . . Fun and play for weeks to come . . . With nothing else to do . . . Than swim and fish and loll around . . . Beneath the heavens blue . . . Yes, even teachers, as they strive . . . For more proficiency . . . By study or by travel, feel . . . That they are much more free . . . And yet in moments all alone . . . They really miss each other . . . The teacher and the little girl . . . And sister's "awful" brother . . . Indeed they will be happy when . . . The schoolbell rings once more . . . And all the youngsters rush again . . . Through that familiar door.

WE CAN'T STAY MAD

I love you so especially . . . When I do something wrong . . . Because you are not able to . . . Stay mad for very long . . . Your disposition seems to be . . . Less human than divine . . . As you forgive and you forget . . . The errors that are mine . . . I never mean to anger you . . . And never, on my part . . . Would I do anything, dear one . . . To really hurt your heart . . . But now and then I make mistakes . . . And it is good to see . . . How kind and understanding and . . . How sweet you are to me . . . And as you are so lovable . . . No wrong that you might do . . . Could make me mad and stay that way . . . For very long at you.

PURSER

The purser is the guardian . . . Aboard an ocean liner . . . Of everyone from tourist to . . . The richest first-class diner . . . Responsible in all respects . . . For comfort and for ease . . . He listens to complaints, and strives . . . In every way to please . . . He is the banker on the waves . . . Including safe deposit . . . For cash and other valuables . . . Entrusted to his closet . . . He pays the crew, and is in charge . . . Of all the personnel . . . And even helps the customs men . . . To see that all goes well . . . The purser is a nurser and an able-bodied tutor . . . Administrator, manager . . . And shipboard trouble-shooter.

NO PRIVATE LIFE

"The Private Life of So-and-So" . . . Or phrased some other way . . . So often is the title of . . . A story or a play . . . And that is most inaccurate . . . As no one walks alone . . . With every second of the day . . . To call his very own . . . There is no private life on earth . . . That could be called complete . . . For there are times when people must . . . Go out upon the street . . . And there are always nosy ones . . . Who dig relentlessly . . . Until they solve the hermit or . . . Secluded family . . . Eventually all privacy . . . Is only temporary . . . As always somebody exhumes . . . The secrets people bury.

BEWARE THE SUNDAY

Beware the Sunday you decide . . . You need not go to church . . . That just a single absence will . . . Not leave you in the lurch . . . Because it only takes one time . . . To weaken your defense . . . Against the possibility . . . Of cold indifference . . . One Sunday missed, and you may feel . . . So careless and so free . . . Another absence will occur . . . Then maybe two or three . . . And then, before you know it, you . . . Are staying home each time . . . Another Sunday morning comes . . . And church bells ring or chime . . . Unless you have a real excuse . . . Too ill or old to go . . . Do worship God each Sunday in . . . The church and faith you know.

IN DOING BUSINESS

Sentiment in business is . . . A serious mistake . . . As it is likely
to reduce . . . The profit that you make . . . That is the view some
people hold . . . And argue to the last . . . Pointing with pride to
all their gains . . . From toughness in the past . . . But how can
they be certain that . . . Their satisfactory score . . . With just a
little sentiment . . . Might not have been much more? . . . One
need not be a softy and . . . Just give his goods away . . . To
each and every customer . . . He deals with every day . . . But
blending business tactics with . . . A kind consideration . . . Can
help his profits grow beyond . . . His fondest expectation.

PROMISE ME, TOO

Dear one, you know I always keep . . . The promises I make . . .
Especially the secret ones . . . For your beloved sake . . . The words
I whisper to your heart . . . That only we may share . . . To promise you with all my heart . . . That I will always care . . . Through
weeks and months, and through the years . . . The thoughts that
I have spoken . . . Have linked a chain of promises . . . That never
has been broken . . . It is a chain I hope that you . . . Will always
wear for me . . . Yes, even in that misty vale . . . Of timeless
memory . . . And in return the only thing . . . I want to ask of
you . . . Is just your loving promise that . . . You also will be true.

LADYBUG

A ladybug is said to be . . . A symbol of good luck . . . As it may
land upon your hand . . . Your table, car or truck . . . It is a lowly
beetle but . . . A lovely creature too . . . As quietly it crawls about
. . . And cuddles up to you . . . And if you do not welcome it . . .
And do not care to play . . . It seems to sense your apathy . . .
And promptly flies away . . . There are those superstitious folks
. . . Who like the ladybug . . . And wish that it were big enough
. . . For them to hold and hug . . . In any case, the ladybug . . .
Presents a certain charm . . . And whether you believe in luck . . .
It cannot do you harm.

HER FRUGAL WAYS

Quite often I have praised my wife . . . For her economy . . . She is
the saving genius of . . . Our loving family . . . But now and then
I do believe . . . She goes a bit too far . . . As when we need a meter-
space . . . In which to park our car . . . She will not take just any
space . . . But we must run around . . . To see what unexpired time
. . . On meters can be found . . . Or if we use a public phone . . .
We drop no money in . . . Until she checks on all the phones . . . In
that returned coin bin . . . And when a dime or parking time . . .
Her happy eye has caught . . . We spend much more for something
. . . We never might have bought.

NO MORE, NO LESS

Each day do only that much which . . . You know that you should do
. . . And there will never be a thing . . . To fret or bother you . . .
Do not extend your efforts to . . . Accomplish more and more . . .
Within those hours of the day . . . To make a higher score . . . Nor
let the precious moments of . . . A single day slip by . . . As tasks
neglected may become . . . A pile that grows too high . . . Too little
or too much at once . . . Is not the very best . . . As lazy ones should
be at work . . . And those who toil should rest . . . Just have an even
schedule, and . . . Fulfill it every day . . . And peace and joy and
true success . . . Will join you on your way.

THY WILL BE DONE

Whenever we ask God to help . . . Ourselves or anyone . . . Our final
words should always be . . . "Thy holy will be done" . . . God hears
the smallest prayer we say . . . And answers each in turn . . . But
sometimes His reply is not . . . The one for which we yearn . . . He
gave us life, and only He . . . Can guide us on our way . . . And only
He can know what things . . . Are best for us today . . . And so if we
petition and . . . Our prayer should be denied . . . It does not mean
that we are shunned . . . And we are turned aside . . . God simply
wills it otherwise . . . As life is lost or won . . . And so each prayer
we ever say . . . Should end, "Thy will be done."

PARTING PARTY

The parting party for a friend . . . When farewell we must say . . . Is
one of handshakes and of smiles . . . While tears are brushed away
. . . It is the time for praise and thanks . . . Perhaps long overdue
. . . For one who did so much for us . . . More than before we knew
. . . More than we realized at the time . . . And therefore could not
see . . . How much that friendship really meant . . . To our com-
munity . . . The parting party is the place . . . To say hello and sigh
. . . And say a fervent prayer that this . . . Is really not good-by . . .
Reminding us there is no need . . . For us to fret or fuss . . . As God
will surely bless our friend . . . And give His grace to us.

RAIN REMINDS ME

Rain reminds me of the tears . . . That fell upon your face . . .
When you and I were meeting at . . . That certain time and place
. . . The tears that flowed the moment when . . . I called you by your
name . . . And made me realize all the more . . . I was the one to
blame . . . I knew that I was guilty and . . . I felt ashamed that night
. . . And I was sorry, darling, I . . . Had brought about your plight
. . . But what you did not know, and I . . . Was just as unaware . . .
You were the only one for whom . . . My heart could really care . . .
And now I have not any doubt . . . Believe me, it is true . . . With
all my heart and all of me . . . I am in love with you.

DECENT JOKES

Funny words from childish lips . . . Are cute as they can be . . . Especially the ones that stir . . . Our childhood memory . . . Little gags
and riddles and . . . Those jokes they like to play . . . Hardly any
different from . . . The ones of yesterday . . . Sometimes we are
stumped, and our . . . Response is really wrong . . . But when we
know the answer, we . . . Act dumb, and go along . . . Because it is
a wholesome way . . . To have a little fun . . . The kind that causes
laughter, and . . . Cannot hurt anyone . . . If only grown-up jokes
and quips . . . Adhered to that same rule . . . There would be fewer
sinful thoughts . . . And less of ridicule.

GOOD ST. PATRICK

If good St. Patrick did no more . . . Than simply to inspire . . . The friendly folks of Ireland with . . . Ambition and desire . . . He would have done sufficiently . . . While he was on this earth . . . To serve almighty God, and be . . . Of everlasting worth . . . But he performed much more than that . . . He helped the poor and weary . . . And lifted many lonely hearts . . . In hours long and dreary . . . And so we honor him today . . . And all the Irish too . . . As they are always cheerful and . . . Devoted, kind and true . . . God bless the Irish everywhere . . . On this St. Patrick's Day . . . Especially the ones who live . . . In our great U.S.A.

NEVER RETIRED

You think you are retired, friend? . . . You could not be more wrong . . . Your every day is active, and . . . Your life should be a song . . . Oh, you may not be quite as quick . . . As once you used to be . . . And you may be a little lame . . . And short of energy . . . But don't you still call people up . . . Or write to some address? . . . Of course you do, and by those deeds . . . You further happiness . . . There is no real retirement . . . For anyone on earth . . . If through the years of smiles and tears . . . His life has proved his worth . . . No, you are not retired—you . . . Are busy at your task . . . Of doing any little thing . . . That anyone may ask.

OFFER A PRAYER

If we would give someone a gift . . . To show how much we care . . . The finest present from the heart . . . Is just to say a prayer . . . A prayer that God will bless that soul . . . And help it on its way . . . With health, success and happiness . . . To reach its goal some day . . . No gift of any worldly goods . . . Can be of equal worth . . . Not all the gold and silver and . . . The diamonds of earth . . . Such riches have no value in . . . The kingdom that is God's . . . (Against our chance of being saved . . . They may increase the odds) . . . But every little prayer we say . . . For someone else's soul . . . Will help that kindred spirit gain . . . Its great, eternal goal.

INVEST IN U.S.

Your wise investment in a stock . . . May bring some good returns
. . . And you may be quite satisfied . . . With what your money earns
. . . Perhaps you have the prospect to . . . Become a millionaire . . .
And all you think about is just . . . The value of a share . . . But
what about a little share . . . Of our good U.S.A.? . . . The best investment anyone . . . Can ever make today? . . . Those savings
bonds that underwrite . . . Our home economy . . . To help the
government insure . . . Our last security . . . For if our nation
should collapse . . . With all its bonds today . . . The value of the
highest stock . . . Would simply melt away.

I RING YOUR PHONE

I called you on the phone, and you . . . Declined to speak to me . . .
Apparently not interested . . . In any memory . . . Apparently you
do not care . . . About the days gone by . . . When once I held you
in my arms . . . And kissed your every sigh . . . You seem to have forgotten all . . . The stars and moons we knew . . . When I assured
you no one else . . . Could mean as much as you . . . Of course it
is your privilege, and . . . The choice is all your own . . . But, oh, I
love you, darling, and . . . I feel so all alone . . . Apparently you do
not care . . . The same as you did then . . . And yet I hope you answer when . . . I ring your phone again.

SPILLED COFFEE

A cup of coffee that is spilled . . . On table or on tray . . . Is never
any reason for . . . Your guests to go away . . . It never should disturb minds . . . Of those who come to call . . . For such a little thing
is no . . . Embarrassment at all . . . Indeed it many times provides
. . . A source of conversation . . . And from the worst monotony
. . . A means of liberation . . . A kitchen towel by the sink . . . Will
quickly soak it up . . . And there will be more coffee hot . . . To
pour into the cup . . . And then you reminisce and laugh . . . About
the days you knew . . . When you were entertained by friends . . .
And spilled your coffee too.

IF YOU WANT FRIENDS

If you would have a faithful friend . . . You have to be one too . . .
And be as good to him as you . . . Would have him be to you . . . For
friendship is a partnership . . . Of true equality . . . Without a doubt,
suspicion or . . . A tinge of jealousy . . . Your friendship tie entitles
you . . . To share his happiness . . . But also you must be prepared
. . . To help him in distress . . . It is the bond of brotherhood . . .
According to God's way . . . By which His children all should live
. . . Their lives from day to day . . . And so as you desire friends . . .
And find them here and there . . . Be sure that in each partnership
. . . You do your equal share.

LAZY SUMMER?

Sometimes summer seems to lag . . . With days so long and warm
. . . Except on those occasions when . . . There is a thunderstorm
. . . Sometimes summer seems to drag . . . The hours are so slow . . .
We wish that it were time again . . . For frosty air and snow . . .
And yet this season has a span . . . The same as all the rest . . . And
if we make the most of it . . . We will be richly blest . . . Summer is
as long or short . . . As we would have it be . . . According to our
laziness . . . Or our activity . . . And if we take advantage of . . .
Each moment of each day . . . Our hearts will soon be wistful that
. . . The summer flew away.

TRUE TO EACH TRUST

Much more than many other things . . . I ever hope to be . . . Is to
be worthy of the trust . . . My friends repose in me . . . For trust is
faith, and faith is love . . . And love is many things . . . Including all
the comfort and . . . The happiness it brings . . . Trust is a badge of
honor that . . . No one can buy or steal . . . It is integrity itself . . .
A truly great ideal . . . The sole foundation, weak or strong . . . For
every floor and wall . . . On which a friendship firmly stands . . .
Or it is bound to fall . . . And so I hope whatever comes . . . Wherever I may be . . . That never once will I betray . . . A trust reposed
in me.

FOR ALL YOUR GIFTS

Thank You, God, for all the gifts . . . That You have given me . . .
For life and health and hope, and for . . . My loving family . . .
Thank You for my neighbors and . . . All other friendships too . . .
And for the soul and mind with which . . . I know and worship You
. . . Thank You for the sunshine and . . . The rain and flowers bright
. . . My opportunity for work . . . And peaceful rest at night . . . I
am truly grateful, God . . . For being on this earth . . . I only wish
that I could be . . . Of more important worth . . . Please help me,
God, to really show . . . Instead of just to say . . . My deep apprecia-
tion of . . . Your blessings every day.

I REALLY DO

I know I cannot offer you . . . Real fame or wealth or such . . . But
I would like to have you know . . . I love you very much . . . I cannot promise you the moon . . . Or anything on earth . . . Except as
I will try to be . . . Of some intrinsic worth . . . But I will cherish
you, my love . . . For all eternity . . . If you will hold me close to
you . . . And really care for me . . . And I will give you everything
. . . Of all I strive to do . . . As long as you are honest, and . . . I
may depend on you . . . And so this message really is . . . To count
the stars above you . . . And let you know in every way . . . How I
sincerely love you.

ROADSIDE INN

I like the quiet roadside inn . . . When shadows shroud the day . . .
And it is time for dinner, as . . . I journey on my way . . . The cottage quaint that somehow seems . . . To be inviting me . . . To
linger there and gaily share . . . Its hospitality . . . The kitchen smells
are heavenly . . . The food is so delicious . . . And in that friendly
atmosphere . . . No movement is suspicious . . . I eat my fill, and I
enjoy . . . The conversation small . . . About the little pleasantries
. . . Acquaintances recall . . . And peacefully I slumber in . . . A
soft and cozy bed . . . With dreamy, roadside memories . . . To keep
me comforted.

T.G.I.F.

Boys and girls have codes to hide . . . The words they want to say . . .
Especially in high school where . . . They strive so hard each day . . .
T.G.I.F. is one of them . . . It comes up every week . . . As they
look forward to the fun . . . And freedom they all seek . . . "Thank
Goodness (now) It's Friday" and . . . Our classes soon will end . . .
With Saturday and Sunday all . . . Our very own to spend . . . Of
course they have their homework but . . . They do not mind too
much . . . Away from classrooms, teachers and . . . From bulletins
and such . . . T.G.I.F. is really just . . . Their simple code to say . . .
Thank goodness for this weekend time . . . To rest, relax and play.

OUR WORLD OF LOVE

I long so much to be with you . . . Each moment of each day . . . I
want so much to be your own . . . In every loving way . . . The sunshine seems to vanish, and . . . The stars all disappear . . . Each time
the clock declares the time . . . When you must leave me, dear . . .
I am so lonely in my heart . . . And I am so afraid . . . That all our
hopes and all our dreams . . . Will be too long delayed . . . Why
must those empty hours pass . . . To shorten life some more . . .
When we could have the whole wide world . . . Right at our feet and
door? . . . No, not the world of fame and wealth . . . Through marvelous seccess . . . But just our own, enormous world . . . Of love and
happiness.

OUR THANKS TO GOD

Let us give humble thanks to God today . . . For all His blessings
good . . . Especially democracy . . . In every neighborhood . . . For
liberty as citizens . . . Regardless of our class . . . However poor we
are, or large . . . The fortune we amass . . . To worship God in our
own way . . . And speak our thoughts out loud . . . And vote as in-
dividuals . . . And not a people cowed . . . Let us be grateful for our
home . . . Our health and happiness . . . For our devoted children,
and . . . Their chances for success . . . And let us give our thanks
to God . . . Whatever we are worth . . . For life and opportunity . . .
To save our souls on earth.

STRANGER-FRIEND

I like the stranger on the street . . . Who waves and says hello . . .
Though he may be somebody I . . . May never get to know . . . It is
that friendly greeting which . . . His heart conveys to me . . . Not to
be funny or polite . . . But in sincerity . . . He merely wants to tell
me that . . . We two are kindred souls . . . As human beings gener-
ally . . . Are seeking self-same goals . . . And every time that happens
I . . . Am tempted to slow down . . . And thereby possibly to find
. . . Another friend in town . . . But always I am hesitant . . . And
bashful when we meet . . . When I might make so many friends . . .
Of strangers on the street.

WHO ARE THE POOR?

There is no shame in being poor . . . No more than there is cause
. . . For any wealthy person to . . . Receive a wide applause . . . The
lack of money does not call . . . For an apology . . . And cash is no
excuse to claim . . . Superiority . . . Because the basic value of . . .
A man upon this earth . . . Is not determined by his fame . . . Or his
financial worth . . . But by his loyalty and faith . . . And his sincerity
. . . And all the other virtues that . . . Comprise integrity . . . No
money and no influence . . . Whatever their amounts . . . Could
ever purchase character . . . The only thing that counts.

WIFE AND MOTHER

What is a wife and mother worth . . . In dollars and in cents? . . .
How high without her help would be . . . Your family expense?
. . . She cooks and cleans and nurses, and . . . She shops for food
and clothes . . . She washes and she irons, and . . . Forever mends
and sews . . . She goes to monthly meetings of . . . The friendly
P.T.A. . . . And helps the eager Cub Scouts and . . . The Brownies
on their way . . . Just think what it would cost you for . . . The services she gives . . . To buy those comforts for the way . . . Your happy
family lives . . . A wife and mother truly is . . . An angel on this
earth . . . And nothing in this life could match . . . Her love and
warmth and worth.

OLD HOMES AND NEW

The home we used to dream of was . . . A cottage small and bright
. . . With flowers fair surrounded by . . . A picket fence of white . . .
But time has changed the scenery . . . As everybody knows . . . And
now there are no cottages . . . Or even bungalows . . . Today they
build those dwellings that . . . Are plain and low and long . . . Designed to be efficient and . . . To look real sound and strong . . .
They call them modern houses and . . . They could not be more right
. . . But to oldtimers they are not . . . A very pleasing sight . . . The
cottages in which they dwelt . . . With happiness and pride . . . Not
only held an inner glow . . . But they looked warm outside.

PUBLIC OPINION

Some people say that publicly . . . Opinion does not matter . . .
And we should just ignore all words . . . Of gossip and of chatter
. . . They say we should not care about . . . What other persons think
. . . Not even if the worst remarks . . . Appear in printer's ink . . .
But their advice is wrong because . . . Opinion can be cruel . . . And
if ignored, it can become . . . The fuel for a duel . . . We should en-
deavor constantly . . . To be above reproach . . . By never doing
anything . . . To harm or to encroach . . . And then if we are men-
aced by . . . Abuse or baneful prattle . . . We should retaliate until
. . . We win the verbal battle.

GO TO SCHOOL

Grade school, high school, college life . . . Whichever it may be . . .
Each day becomes another one . . . To keep in memory . . . Sitting
in the classroom may . . . Not be exactly pleasant . . . But you want
education, and . . . You're glad that you are present . . . And so
eventually you learn . . . The things you want to know . . . To help
your mind and morals and . . . Your character to grow . . . School is
truly wonderful . . . It broadens brain and vision . . . Especially in
guiding you . . . To make the right decision . . . Do go to school if
you have time . . . No matter what your age . . . Your knowledge
will be greater with . . . The turning of each page.

ENJOY YOUR BABY

Your baby is quite little now . . . But he will soon grow up . . . To occupy his chair so high . . . And slurp from his own cup . . . And he will start to crawl around . . . And walk before you know it . . . And as he bites the furniture . . . His teeth marks sure will show it . . . And when he learns to talk, you'll wish . . . He never had his say . . . As he will ask a thousand things . . . You can't explain away . . . Then suddenly your boy will sprout . . . In body and in knowledge . . . And you'll discover that he is . . . Prepared to go to college . . . So keep your baby while you can . . . And feed him with a spoon . . . A little one is precious but . . . He grows up all too soon.

OUR EQUAL CHANCE

We go along from day to day . . . And then we are surprised . . . As someone is promoted or . . . His vessel has capsized . . . And yet there is no reason for . . . Our minds to be amazed . . . Or by some other sudden change . . . To feel the least bit dazed . . . In other countries there may be . . . Real cause for consternation . . . Or as the wheel of fortune turns . . . There may be celebration . . . But here in our United States . . . It is a normal thing . . . To stake and take our fortune as . . . The pendulum may swing . . . For life is always changing, and . . . As we may lose today . . . Tomorrow may bring victory . . . Along our equal way.

YOUR ONLY VALUE

What is the value of your life? . . . What does it mean to you? . . . The chance to strive for comfort and . . . To make your dreams come true? . . . To harvest happiness on earth . . . Wherever it may be . . . And maybe gain a golden fame . . . For future history? . . . Then you are selfish in your heart . . . And wrong in your desire . . . Because your motive should be on . . . A level so much higher . . . The real and only value of . . . Your life depends today . . . On how you serve your neighbor in . . . Your most unselfish way . . . The only, lasting value of . . . Your life upon this sod . . . Is not how happy you may be . . . But how you honor God.

WE STILL NEED DIMES

So many are our charities . . . We cannot help but feel . . . That possibly some begging hands . . . Are not exactly real . . . And possibly there is some fraud . . . (It does occur sometimes) . . . But never is there any doubt . . . About our March of Dimes . . . No dime is ever wasted, as . . . It helps our research grow . . . To aid our suffering patients, and . . . To stamp out polio . . . The new vaccine is wonderful . . . As any drug can be . . . And certainly it will protect . . . The average family . . . But dimes are still in great demand . . . To help that research flow . . . So do be generous as you . . . Consider polio.

I DREAM TO SLEEP

I cannot sleep unless I dream . . . Of you, my dearest one . . . And so my rest depends on you . . . When every day is done . . . My rest depends on whether you . . . Are still in love with me . . . And I am certain that you are . . . As happy as can be . . . If ever any day or night . . . You gave me cause to doubt . . . I could not close my eyes, for I . . . Would toss and turn about . . . Thanks be to God that every night . . . I sleep the stars away . . . And I awake with strength renewed . . . To meet another day . . . And thanks to you, my dearest one . . . Because you are so true . . . For I could never go to sleep . . . Without sweet dreams of you.

LITTLE GIRL'S DOLLY

A little girl is happy with . . . A dolly all her own . . . It is such pleasant company . . . She seldom feels alone . . . She cuddles it and coos to it . . . And sees that it is fed . . . And when the evening star appears . . . She tucks it into bed . . . Not many babies in this life . . . Receive more tender care . . . As "little mother" dresses it . . . And combs its curly hair . . . She watches over dolly, and . . . She guides it on its way . . . By teaching it the meaning of . . . The things that grown-ups say . . . And when a new one comes along . . . Though she will cherish it . . . Her first-born dolly usually . . . Remains her favorite.

RED CROSS FOR ALL

The Red Cross is no arbiter . . . And it does not take sides . . . It
serves the world, as mercy calls . . . When tragic are the tides . . .
It matters not what flag may fly . . . Or what the race or creed . . .
But just that there is suffering . . . And there is desperate need . . .
Tornado, flood or fire in . . . The land that is our own . . . Or
wounded soldiers overseas . . . So painful and alone . . . The Red
Cross is for everyone . . . For all humanity . . . And much of its suc-
cess depends . . . Upon our charity . . . Our willingness and readiness
. . . To help our brothers live . . . With all the blood donations
and . . . The money we can give.

SHARE YOUR GLORY

There is no project on this earth . . . That you can do alone . . . No
deed, however great or small . . . That you may call your own . . .
For always there is someone else . . . Or two or three or more . . .
Without whose help you never would . . . Have made so high a score
. . . You may put over civic drives . . . Or those for charity . . . But
you are helped by volunteers . . . Who work so willingly . . . And
even if the project is . . . Exclusively for you . . . Some others indirectly help . . . In what you strive to do . . . If just a smile or friendly
word . . . One moment of today . . . You have to share your glory
with . . . Each boost along the way.

WHO NEVER PRAY

Some people never think of God . . . As long as skies are bright . . .
Their health is good, and everything . . . Appears to be all right . . .
They do not go to church because . . . They simply do not care . . .
And feel it would be wasting time . . . To say the smallest prayer
. . . Why should they pray, when they have all . . . They struggled
to possess . . . And by their own ability . . . Achieved their great
success? . . . They live a dangerous, foolish life . . . For there may
come a day . . . When in their desperate need for help . . . They
know not how to pray . . . And even if they never have . . . A set-
back on this sod . . . How, in the end, can they explain . . . Their
selfishness to God?

BACK TO THE GRIND

Few things are quite as difficult . . . As getting back in stride . . .
When we must go to work again . . . And put our play aside . . .
When our vacation days are spent . . . And mountain, lake and sea
. . . Have somehow suddenly become . . . A dreamy memory . . .
The freedom and the laughter of . . . The time that was our own
. . . With never any clock to punch . . . Or discipline by phone . . .
And yet there is no reason good . . . For us to feel that way . . . We
knew and we agreed that we . . . Would have to face this day . . .
Relaxed, refreshed, we should exude . . . A cheerfulness sincere . . .
To do good work and so insure . . . More holidays next year.

SO GLAD IT HAPPENED

The happiest of happenings . . . That ever happened, dear . . . Was
meeting you and seeing you . . . So charming and sincere . . . Perhaps it merely happened, as . . . The world may well agree . . . But
I would like to think that God . . . Intended it to be . . . Because I
felt, my darling, when . . . I first set eyes on you . . . You were my
one, my only one . . . No other one would do . . . It happened that
I met you—yes . . . And life became a song . . . And yet somehow
it seemed that I . . . Had known you all along . . . But now it really
matters not . . . By chance or by design . . . I give my thanks to
God and you . . . That you are truly mine.

YOUR SIGNATURE

Your signature on anything . . . Becomes a promise true . . . To certify a bargain closed . . . Or something you will do . . . A contract
for your labor or . . . A deed to certain land . . . Or any note that
must be paid . . . In time or on demand . . . Yes, even on a letter
when . . . You merely greet a friend . . . It stands for your sincereness
in . . . The message that you send . . . Your signature is valuable
. . . Or it is worthless now . . . Accordingly as you are one . . . To
keep or break a vow . . . In any case, remember that . . . Whatever
you may do . . . When signing any document . . . Your signature is
you.

THANK YOU, DARLING

Happy birthday, darling, and . . . My gratitude to you . . . For all
your smiles and all you have . . . Inspired me to do . . . Thank you
for the loving help . . . That you have given me . . . Thank you for
our children and . . . Each happy memory . . . Thank you for your
kindness and . . . Your understanding way . . . So tenderly forgiving
me . . . My faults from day to day . . . Thank you for each sacrifice
. . . So like a silent prayer . . . And all the goodness of yourself . . .
That you have let me share . . . Thank you, darling, and may God
. . . Enable me to do . . . My very best to bring the best . . . Of happiness to you.

STAMP OF APPROVAL

There are so many different stamps . . . Around the world today . . .
The ones we have to buy and those . . . The merchants give away
. . . The stamps to mail our letters or . . . The circulars we send . . .
Or packages by parcel post . . . To customer or friend . . . The
stamps that promise discounts on . . . Some purchases we make . . .
Including certain magazines . . . We may decide to take . . . And
then there are the rubber stamps . . . We ink and gently press . . .
And those that are the human kind . . . Who only answer "yes" . . .
But more important in this life . . . Than any other one . . . Is that
which stamps approval on . . . A worthy deed well done.

SUSTAIN US, GOD

Merciful God, forgive our sins . . . And bless our souls today . . .
Give us the grace and strength we need . . . To live a better way
. . . Let not our sunshine disappear . . . Let not our hearts despair
. . . But keep us, God, forever in . . . Your kind and loving care . . .
Show us the way to heaven on . . . The right and narrow path . . .
And help us to avoid the wrongs . . . That would deserve Your wrath
. . . Be with us from the break of dawn . . . Until the shadows fall
. . . And through the night protect us with . . . Your warm and holy
shawl . . . Give us Your bread of life, dear God . . . Sustain us in our
needs . . . Forgive our faults and credit our . . . Sincere and honest
deeds.

ACT FRIENDLY

However sad, discouraging . . . Or dark may be your mood . . . You should greet other people with . . . A friendly attitude . . . Yes, even if you must pretend . . . That nothing has gone wrong . . . That you are filled with happiness . . . And life is like a song . . . Your smile will hide your ugly mood . . . And it will be untrue . . . But it will comfort friends and be . . . Good medicine for you . . . Because as you help others, you . . . Will find a certain cure . . . For all the tribulations that . . . You think you must endure . . . Look happy and be neighborly . . . With every word you say . . . And God will bless your loving soul . . . And take your fears away.

SO HARD TO WAIT

I know we have to wait, my love . . . But in so many ways . . . I find it difficult to bide . . . The months, the weeks, the days . . . Because I keep remembering . . . That life is just a while . . . And it can be as fleeting as . . . The flicker of a smile . . . Our life together could go on . . . For years and years on end . . . In which to share a paradise . . . Where dreams and beauty blend . . . And yet for us this world, my love . . . Could end quite suddenly . . . Indeed it might occur before . . . You could belong to me . . . It is so difficult to wait . . . To hear your promise true . . . Because I want as much of life . . . As I can be with you.

BILLFOLD PHOTO

No billfold ever is complete . . . Unless somewhere inside . . . There is a little picture of . . . The owner's special pride . . . The fiancée who fills the dreams . . . Of one in ecstasy . . . The loving spouse, the baby new . . . Or all the family . . . Whatever else the billfold holds . . . That photo must be there . . . And frequently it is displayed . . . With pride and tender care . . . It is a greater treasure than . . . The greenbacks, side by side . . . The cards of membership or those . . . Of credit certified . . . New cards replace expired ones . . . And cash goes out each day . . . But that important photograph . . . Is right in there to stay.

DO NOT HURRY

I really hurt my forehead with . . . A sudden, thoughtless caper . . .
As I stepped out upon the porch . . . To get the daily paper . . .
Dressed in my slippers and my robe . . . I did not want to be . . . A
sight extraordinary for . . . My neighbors all to see . . . There really
was no reason for . . . The way I hurried then . . . And now I hope
I never shall . . . Be quite so quick again . . . For when I dashed
out there, and jumped . . . To scurry back inside . . . My forehead
hit the doorway, and . . . I thought I nearly died . . . The blood kept
streaming down my face . . . And I had cause to worry . . . But I
recovered, and I learned . . . My lesson not to hurry.

LOVE ME, MY DARLING

I promise all of me to you . . . As long as life goes on . . . Until the
setting of that sun . . . When everything is gone . . . All that I have
is yours to hold . . . Your own on earth forever . . . My hopes and
dreams, my words and deeds . . . My vow to leave you never . . . I
promise you with all my heart . . . You are the only one . . . The
greatest prize in all the world . . . I ever could have won . . . You are
the only one for me . . . The only one I cherish . . . Without your
arms around me, dear . . . I think that I would perish . . . My darling, please accept my heart . . . And give yourself to me . . . With
every fond embrace and kiss . . . To hold in memory.

WHAT IS A BLESSING?

What is a blessing in this life? . . . It is a kindly nod . . . The sunshine of a special smile . . . Bestowed on us by God . . . As blessing
is the timely hand . . . That stays calamity . . . Or keeps us calm and
sensible . . . When there is tragedy . . . It is each rung we reach upon
. . . Our ladder to success . . . And everything along our way . . .
That brings us happiness . . . A blessing is our loving spouse . . .
The baby in our arms . . . And life itself upon this earth . . . With all
its dreams and charms . . . Each blessing means so very much . . .
We should take time to say . . . A prayer of gratitude to God . . . For
helping us each day.

TRY LOVING MONDAY

Try to love each Monday new . . . And you will make the grade . . .
For Monday is that grouchy time . . . When most affections fade
. . . Somehow that is when the world . . . Is in a nasty mood . . .
And human conduct has a way . . . Of being rather rude . . . If you
can conquer Monday, you . . . Are headed for success . . . With love
and friendship all throughout . . . A week of happiness . . . Have a
pleasant feeling when . . . The working days begin . . . To make you
happier by far . . . And likelier to win . . . Try to love each Monday
with . . . A heart sincere and true . . . And never will you ever
know . . . A Monday that is blue.

OUR HONEST WORDS

Grownups cogitate upon . . . The words they plan to state . . .
But children bother not the least . . . And never hesitate . . . Youngsters blurt out unabashed . . . The thoughts they have in mind . . .
Which may be complimentary . . . Or possibly unkind . . . They do
not mean to praise or hurt . . . With words that they declare . . .
They simply speak instinctively . . . To people everywhere . . . And
many are the lessons that . . . We learn from day to day . . . By
listening to the little ones . . . And what they have to say . . . Especially that teaching which . . . We had in early youth . . . To live
a life of honesty . . . And always tell the truth.

NIGHT WORK

Some people labor through the day . . . While others work at night
. . . As dawn or dark may be their choice . . . Or it may be their
plight . . . Of course, most people like to sleep . . . When stars are in
the sky . . . They feel that daytime slumber keeps . . . More beauty
from the eye . . . Or they may think that they miss out . . . On more
important things . . . As daylight seems to emphasize . . . The joy
that living brings . . . But God made night, as well as day . . . And
as the world goes on . . . Each moment is important in . . . The dark
the same as dawn . . . So let us not surrender to . . . The smallest
doubt or fright . . . If sometime it should happen that . . . We have
to work at night.

GIVE DADDY CREDIT

No daddy new should be condemned . . . For his paternal pride . . .
For, after all, he paced the floor . . . Before the baby cried . . . And
after that he paced the floor . . . Of every room at home . . . Whenever there was any need . . . For lullabies to roam . . . He had to pay
the hospital . . . And pay the doctor too . . . And foot the bills for
rent and food . . . And little garments new . . . He had to purchase
those cigars . . . And try to get a raise . . . To keep his dignity the
while . . . His wife got all the praise . . . Yes, she was very wonderful
. . . God bless her loving heart . . . But, after all, the daddy new . . .
Did play some little part.

TO LIVE FOR GOD

Thank You, God, for yesternight . . . And thank You for today
. . . And every chance we have to live . . . According to Your way
. . . Thank You for each second of . . . The breath of life on earth
. . . As it may give us time in which . . . To prove our human
worth . . . We do not mean to hurt You, God . . . With sins that we
commit . . . Each wrong is one more failure, and . . . It makes us
more unfit . . . But we are sorry for our wrongs . . . And beg forgiving
grace . . . Absolving us and helping in . . . The problems we must
face . . . Forgive us for our failure, God . . . And help our hearts
be true . . . As now we promise faithfully . . . To live our lives for
You.

POOR PRETZEL

Poor Pretzel broke a paw-nail, and . . . You never saw such fuss . . .
Until we got him to the "vet" . . . Who patched him up for us . . .
Although our dachshund lost some blood . . . And must have suf-
fered pain . . . He did not whine or quiver or . . . In any way com-
plain . . . And that is just like Pretzel, who . . . Has every battle scar
. . . From canine fights to having been . . . Run over by a car . . .
As one good neighbor said to us . . . His life has sure been hard . . .
And yet his constant courage is . . . A virtue to regard . . . Poor Pret-
zel is a precious dog . . . So brave and very smart . . . And for his
wounds he ought to get . . . A special Purple Heart.

FRIENDS ON EARTH

Friends can be so helpful and . . . So wonderful to know . . . If only when they take the time . . . To call and say hello . . . Just the knowledge that they care . . . And that they think of you . . . Can really help you do your best . . . In all you strive to do . . . To know that you are wanted and . . . You feel that you belong . . . Can banish any doubt you have . . . And make your life a song . . . Friends are angels who give faith . . . And hope and strength to you . . . To carry on from day to day . . . And make your dreams come true . . . Only God can help you more . . . Than all your friends on earth . . . As He created all of them . . . And He allowed your birth.

THE RIVER FLOWS

There are things to remember and things to forget . . . In the world of our yesterdays . . . But only to guide us, inspire or chide us . . . As we journey our separate ways . . . The moments of pleasure we wanted to treasure . . . So good to recall now and then . . . And every mistake that we hope for our sake . . . We never will make again . . . While losses and sorrows and hopeless tomorrows . . . Should never re-enter the mind . . . The slightest complexion of fear or dejection . . . Is better to leave behind . . . There are things to remember and things to forget . . . As a Hindu said long ago . . . There is never a day as we go on our way . . . We can ever continue to know . . . We never can bathe in the same river twice . . . Whatever may be its name . . . For the river flows on and on and on . . . And the water is never the same.

WHAT TO WEAR

Some people like the latest styles . . . In all the clothes they wear . . . And make each new selection with . . . The greatest thought and care . . . No matter what the cost may be . . . They have to look their best . . . According to the articles . . . That meet the fashion test . . . While others put on garments that . . . Were common yesterday . . . Not new in any sense but still . . . Too good to throw away . . . Replacements may cost more than what . . . Their budgets will allow . . . Or maybe they prefer the clothes . . . That they are wearing now . . . Some people judge appearance by . . . The latest fashion book . . . While others are content with just . . . That neat and tidy look.

GOOD TO BE HOME

When you must travel far and wide . . . By air or ocean foam . . .
The moment that is happiest . . . Is that of getting home . . . To be
back with your family . . . And safely in your nest . . . Relax your
muscles and your bones . . . And have a well-earned rest . . . To
saunter on the sidewalk and . . . To see old friends again . . . Who
are as good and wonderful . . . As you remember when . . . Somehow familiar faces and . . . The places that you knew . . . Recall the
sweetest memories . . . To please and comfort you . . . Some joy
will always be with you . . . Wherever you may roam . . . But, oh,
it is so wonderful . . . And good to be back home.

REMIND ME, GOD

Dear God, when I am lonely, and . . . Perhaps I feel despair . . .
Let not my ailing heart forget . . . That You hear every prayer . . .
Remind me that no matter what . . . I do or fail to do . . . There
still is hope for me as long . . . As I have faith in You . . . Let not
my eyes be blinded by . . . Some folly I commit . . . But help me
to regret my wrong . . . And to make up for it . . . Inspire me to put
my fears . . . Upon a hidden shelf . . . And in the future never to
. . . Be sorry for myself . . . Give me the restful sleep I need . . .
Before another dawn . . . And bless me in the morning with . . .
The courage to go on.

OUR REAL UMBRELLA

Friendship is a priceless thing . . . As people live and die . . . More
valuable than money and . . . All goods that it can buy . . . Friendship in the sunshine or . . . The fiercest storm at night . . . Friendship at a funeral . . . With prayer and candlelight . . . It is the dear
companionship . . . That helps us celebrate . . . Or sympathizes
when we meet . . . A most unfortunate fate . . . Friendship is a
passkey to . . . Forgiveness or reprieve . . . More surely than material
wealth . . . Our suffering could relieve . . . Friendship true is faith
and trust . . . And eagerness to aid . . . Our real umbrella when we
might . . . Feel lonely or afraid.

MIDWINTER

Midwinter seems a dreary time . . . When holidays are spent . . .
And sometimes we are given to . . . Be downright discontent . . .
We do not like the gloomy sky . . . The snow and ice and sleet . . .
The barren trees, the frozen ground . . . That lies beneath our feet
. . . But every year is just so long . . . And every season, too . . .
And always it requires time . . . To make our dreams come true . . .
As surely as each dawn appears . . . To end another night . . . So
there will be another spring . . . With hope and beauty bright . . .
Midwinter can be beautiful . . . It makes some people glad . . . And
as for those who like it not . . . Well, it is just too bad.

YOUR GIFT AND MINE

I treasure all the presents dear . . . That you have given me . . . But,
most of all, the one you placed . . . Beneath our Christmas tree . . .
It did not cost you anything . . . In terms of money spent . . . But
it is priceless as a gift . . . Of loving sentiment . . . No article of
luxury . . . But just a little note . . . A message of affection, dear
. . . That you sincerely wrote . . . It simply said, "I love you," and
. . . It was addressed to me . . . Which made your Christmas present, dear . . . My own exclusively . . . I thank you, darling, and I
hope . . . You liked my present too . . . As I embraced you and I
said . . . Those very words to you.

PAYING GUEST

When someone is invited to . . . A banquet as a guest . . . He should
not have to buy his meal . . . The same as all the rest . . . And usually
he need not fear . . . That such will be the case . . . But now and
then that is the shock . . . Which he is forced to face . . . It is astonishing how crude . . . Some would-be host can be . . . How lacking
in good manners and . . . In common courtesy . . . The price per
plate is not what counts . . . However large or small . . . But just that
any guest should be . . . Allowed to pay at all . . . It causes one to
hesitate . . . With righteous indignation . . . Before agreeing to accept . . . Another invitation.

HAPPY FAMILY

A family is happy when . . . It really gets along . . . And children grow in character . . . And spiritually strong . . . When everyone co-operates . . . To keep the golden rule . . . As feelings are respected, and . . . There is no ridicule . . . What is the good of arguing . . . Or bickering all day? . . . And why should there be jealousy . . . To turn the heart away? . . . True love is not just tolerance . . . In living side by side . . . But each success should always be . . . A cause for common pride . . . A family is happy when . . . It shares the daily weather . . . Of work and recreation, and . . . It goes to church together.

TO MEAN A PRAYER

A prayer can be so meaningless . . . If we do not believe . . . That we have any chance to get . . . The gift we would receive . . . We cannot simply challenge God . . . To make our dream come true . . . By uttering a printed prayer . . . However old or new . . . We must have faith that God will hear . . . Our very special plea . . . And our approach to Him must be . . . In all humility . . . And also we must be resigned . . . To His most holy will . . . As he accepts or He rejects . . . Some favor to fulfill . . . A prayer can bring no real results . . . Unless we make it clear . . . With faith, humility and hope . . . In every sense sincere.

BLESS ALL WHO SERVE

God, give Your kindly blessing to . . . Our veterans today . . . To all who wore the uniform . . . Of our great U.S.A. . . . To all who served in war or peace . . . At home or overseas . . . To guard our freedom-loving shore . . . Against our enemies . . . And pour Your special blessings, God . . . On every cross that stands . . . Above a hero's lonely grave . . . In strange and distant lands . . . Be good to them, and give us strength . . . To fight for what is right . . . Whenever some aggressor tries . . . To rule the world with might . . . Bless all our veterans today . . . Let every struggle cease . . . And grant that those who gave their all . . . Forever rest in peace.

THANK GOD, AND PRAY

Let us appreciate all gifts . . . That God has brought our way . . .
And give our special thanks to Him . . . On this Thanksgiving Day
. . . For life and promise in a land . . . Of opportunity . . . And all
the joys we share each day . . . With our dear family . . . Let us be
grateful for our health . . . And for our friendship true . . . So many
times so helpful in . . . The things we strive to do . . . As well as all
compatriots . . . Forever at our side . . . To help us guard our liberty
. . . With courage and with pride . . . And let us pray that in this
world . . . Of rivalry intense . . . Humanity, despite its greed . . .
May keep its common sense.

TO GO TO SLEEP

Sometimes I try to go to sleep . . . In dreams of long ago . . . The
places and the faces of . . . The world I used to know . . . Not as
they really happened but . . . The way I wish they had . . . With
everything quite wonderful . . . And nothing very sad . . . They are
the day-dreams that I have . . . When I am snug in bed . . . Unmindful of tomorrow and . . . Realities ahead . . . I make up every happy
scene . . . I wish I could be in . . . Although I know that in the past
. . . It never could have been . . . It may seem foolish, and my
thoughts . . . May not be very deep . . . But I am more than grateful
if . . . It helps me get to sleep.

SUGGESTION BOX

There is a box more valuable . . . Than many other kinds . . . Because it holds the thinking of . . . Alert, ingenious minds . . . The
box in which suggestions are . . . Invited to be dropped . . . For
practices to be improved . . . Or those that should be stopped . . .
In office, store and factory . . . It welcomes notions new . . . For
what may be a better or . . . A brilliant thing to do . . . And usually
rewards are made . . . By bonus or by raise . . . To those whose good
ideas deserve . . . Some words of special praise . . . However young
the worker, or . . . Unknown may be his name . . . One bright sug-
gestion may become . . . His rise to wealth and fame.

RIDE HOME

When I am going home from work . . . With strength and patience tried . . . I am so grateful to the friend . . . Who offers me a ride . . . Not for the bus or taxi fare . . . I need not spend that day . . . Or for that transportation which . . . Provides a smoother way . . . But just because such thoughtfulness . . . Means ever so much more . . . As he takes special care of me . . . And brings me to my door . . . And for the conversation good . . . That fills the friendly air . . . With dreams of happy times ahead . . . We plan to have and share . . . My heart is truly grateful for . . . The comfort of that ride . . . But most of all because I have . . . A real friend at my side.

TO SEE OURSELVES

God, help us to behold ourselves . . . Not by our brightest star . . . As we may seem to others now . . . But as we really are . . . Help us to analyze our worth . . . With thinking that is sound . . . And so be certain that we keep . . . Our feet upon the ground . . . And thereby never to forget . . . That all great deeds we do . . . And every claim we have to fame . . . Belong at last to You . . . There is no problem on this earth . . . That we could ever face . . . Or any dream that could come true . . . Without Your loving grace . . . So help us, God, to serve You well . . . And draw a little nearer . . . As humbly we appraise ourselves . . . When we look in a mirror.

WHO HAS HOMEWORK?

Some school-age youngsters do not like . . . The homework they must do . . . Because it seems for evermore . . . Before their task is through . . . But they have little reason to . . . Complain upon that score . . . As parents have their homework, and . . . Indeed a whole lot more . . . Not just the job of keeping house . . . Preparing meals and such . . . And blessing every moment with . . . That fond, familiar touch . . . But also all that homework when . . . The youngsters are asleep . . . Especially the budget that . . . The parents try to keep . . . And also, more importantly . . . Their plans and dreams each night . . . To help their children on their way . . . Where they will turn out right.

OUR 28TH

Another anniversary . . . Is ours to share today . . . Our eight and
twenty years, my love . . . Along our married way . . . I love you, and
I thank you for . . . Whatever small success . . . I may have gathered
to support . . . And bring you happiness . . . I thank you for the
faith and hope . . . That you have given me . . . And for that greatest
joy of all . . . Our charming children three . . . I thank you for your
management . . . Of family affairs . . . And for your patient shoulder-
ing . . . Of, oh, so many cares . . . A thousand times I thank you, love
. . . For all our dreams come true . . . As long as there is life in me
. . . My heart will cherish you.

MAKE UP YOUR MIND

Why do you keep me wondering? . . . Why are your lips so still? . . .
Why do you hesitate, dear one . . . To say you won't or will? . . . I
know, of course, you have the right . . . To take your time in this
. . . The same as you may hesitate . . . To let me have a kiss . . . But
everyone gets tired when . . . He has to wait and wait . . . For somebody to turn him down . . . Or set a special date . . . It can't go on
forever, as . . . The wheel of fortune turns . . . No matter how de-
votedly . . . And lovingly he yearns . . . And as, no doubt, you want
your life . . . To be a happy song . . . There has to be a limit on . . .
The time I go along.

WRITE UNTO OTHERS

Sometimes you are so lonely that . . . You seem to reach the end . . .
And then you suddenly receive . . . A letter from a friend . . . An
unexpected letter from . . . A friend you seldom met . . . Someone
who knew you casually . . . But who did not forget . . . And as you
read each word and line . . . You feel a whole lot better . . . And you
thank God Almighty for . . . So comforting a letter . . . It is a blessing wonderful . . . That should remind your heart . . . To keep in
touch with all your friends . . . However far apart . . . And to remind
you even more . . . Of how much you can do . . . By writing to the
ones who hope . . . To get some help from you.

A MOTHER'S TIME

Some husbands think their wives have quite . . . An easy time of it
. . . And there is never an excuse . . . For them to throw a fit . . .
They feel their wives deprive themselves . . . Of pleasure and of play
. . . Because they do not organize . . . Their hours of the day . . .
But how can mothers regulate . . . The time when babies cry . . .
And when the phone or doorbell rings . . . And they are forced to fly?
. . . They clean the house and make the beds . . . And in all tasks
are steady . . . While hoping husbands will come home . . . When
they have dinner ready . . . Perhaps the wife without a child . . .
Could well be criticized . . . But mothers do not have the time . . .
That can be organized.

TO WIPE THE SLATE

Each Sunday is another page . . . That fills my memory book . . .
Where I remember God again . . . And take a backward look . . .
And there I see the record of . . . My very early youth . . . When
everything was beautiful . . . And every word was truth . . . And
then I turn another page . . . And I am growing up . . . And there
is bitterness as well . . . As sweetness in my cup . . . The days and
years go by, and now . . . It is quite clear to me . . . What I decide
to do is my . . . Responsibility . . . I wish I were a child again . . .
And did not have to think . . . And all my sins were written down
. . . In disappearing ink.

OUR PICTURE

The camera takes a picture and . . . The picture cannot lie . . . It has
to be exactly as . . . It met the camera's eye . . . But how about the
picture we . . . Present from day to day . . . That ought to be a like-
ness true . . . Of what we think and say? . . . Are we as honest and
as good . . . As we appear to be . . . Or do we stoop to phony and
. . . To trick photography? . . . Yes, we can hide our selfishness . . .
And hatred with a smile . . . And camouflage in other ways . . . But
only for a while . . . Though we may pass around a print . . . Of how
we seem to live . . . Someday it will be known that we . . . Touched
up the negative.

TOUGH POLICE

Some people think police are tough . . . And they are fairly right . . .
As law officials must be stern . . . And brave enough to fight . . .
But that is not a natural trait . . . Of those with badge and gun . . .
And doing what they have to do . . . Is anything but fun . . . Their
duty is to guard our lives . . . And strive in every way . . . To keep
the least offense or crime . . . From happening today . . . So, when
a felony occurs . . . They must pursue each lead . . . Suspecting all
who might have been . . . Connected with the deed . . . They have
to find each criminal . . . Who played the smallest part . . . But
underneath that scowl and badge . . . There beats a human heart.

BEWARE OF PAYDAY

A great mistake is one we make . . . When payday comes around
. . . As we have been quite broke, and now . . . Our pocketbooks
abound . . . We feel exhilarated by . . . The cash we have on hand
. . . And we are quite prepared to meet . . . A payment on demand
. . . We figure there is cause today . . . To celebrate a bit . . . (Forget about tomorrow—there . . . Is time enough for it) . . . And so
we pay up only those . . . That are the urgent bills . . . And all
too soon again we have . . . Our economic ills . . . A paycheck is no
license for . . . A sudden spending spree . . . It should be wisely
budgeted . . . For all the family.

WONDERFUL PEOPLE

Some people find real happiness . . . When other folks are glad . . .
And sorrow when their friends have cause . . . To be the least bit sad
. . . They sympathize in worries and . . . Rejoice in happiness . . .
As others have their troubles or . . . Achieve some new success . . .
They are the people wonderful . . . Of kindred spirit true . . . So
interested in everything . . . Their friends and neighbors do . . .
Not nosy in the slightest way . . . But honest and sincere . . . As
they wish everybody else . . . The very best of cheer . . . And with
that charity of heart . . . They never feel alone . . . While smaller
grow the problems that . . . Appear to be their own.

BABY NEEDS BOTH

A baby needs both parents' care . . . To be real well and strong . . .
Dear Mommy first, but Daddy too . . . To help it get along . . .
The mother gives that tender care . . . With hugs and kisses sweet
. . . And all the comforts of a home . . . Good food and clothes so
neat . . . The father earns the daily bread . . . For all the family
. . . He pays the bills, and he invests . . . For their security . . . Dear
Mommy washes, irons, and . . . She keeps the house so clean . . .
But Daddy also is a part . . . Of that domestic scene . . . He has to
make real sure, among . . . A lot of other things . . . That Baby is
not tied too fast . . . To Mommy's apron strings.

TRY NOT HIS PATIENCE

Be not discouraged when the way . . . Is weary where you plod . . .
But keep your faith and hope in life . . . Lift up your heart to God
. . . Confess the sins that weigh your soul . . . And ask Him for His
aid . . . And fear not now how small may be . . . The progress you
have made . . . God understands how weak you are . . . The same
as everyone . . . And He will not condemn you for . . . The wrongs
that you have done . . . As long as you believe in Him . . . And
struggle every day . . . To make amends and try to live . . . According to His way . . . But do not put your efforts off . . . Until it is too
late . . . Who knows the limit of how long . . . Almighty God will
wait?

WE LOVE YOU, DON

We love you, Don, for nineteen years . . . That you have been on
earth . . . As we have always loved you from . . . The moment of
your birth . . . A very happy birthday and . . . Congratulations, son
. . . For college credits and for all . . . The merits you have won . . .
We wish you all the best in life . . . That you can ever get . . . With
never any doubtful day . . . Or moment of regret . . . Keep up your
faith and courage in . . . Your struggle and your strife . . . And be
forever loyal to . . . Your principles in life . . . Congratulations, Don,
and may . . . You gain the highest score . . . As every day in every
way . . . We love you more and more.

LANDLUBBER

He is the one as ignorant . . . Of sailing as can be . . . Who may
have traveled far on land . . . But does not know the sea . . . He
does not know the flying jib . . . The mizzen sail or main . . . Or
how to haul the boom, and tack . . . To challenge wind and rain . . .
His legs are somewhat wobbly on . . . The swaying, rolling deck . . .
And usually his stomach will . . . Be up around his neck . . . But
always he is welcome, if . . . He wants to come aboard . . . And he is
given every chance . . . To win his great reward . . . And if he finds
his sea legs, and . . . Comes safely back to shore . . . Landlubber
once he may have been . . . But now he is no more.

HAPPY NEW YEAR

A Happy New Year, one and all . . . May God be good to you . . .
And as you strive sincerely now . . . May all your dreams come true
. . . May all your loved ones have the best . . . Of everything this
year . . . Success, good health, a share of wealth . . . And worlds of
friendly cheer . . . May all your troubles disappear . . . And may
you have no more . . . As you endeavor every day . . . To make a
higher score . . . These wishes come right from the heart . . . But do
remember now . . . That God will bless you only as . . . You keep
your smallest vow . . . So do be honest with yourself . . . And everyone you know . . And this will be your finest year . . . Wherever
you may go.

A FRIEND RETURNS

Friends go by, and years go by . . . Then suddenly you meet . . .
And say a fond hello again . . . Along a certain street . . . Friends
whose faces and whose names . . . You long have left behind . . .
Who suddenly come back to life . . . To stir your hazy mind . . .
And so you see each other, and . . . At least you are polite . . . If
just to ask, "How is your health?" . . . And "Have you been all right?"
. . . But now and then an old-time friend . . . Means just a little
more . . . And friendship is a vanished ship . . . Returning to your
shore . . . And though it may not ever be . . . The same as it was
then . . . It is so good and wonderful . . . To see that one again.

WE STILL OWE GOD

There is no freedom from all debts . . . However much we pay . . .
For there is always what we owe . . . Almighty God today . . . We
cannot ever pay Him back . . . For life upon this earth . . . And for
His grace and all the strength . . . We need to prove our worth . . .
His love and His protection for . . . Our home and family . . . And
all His other gifts to reach . . . His great eternity . . . He gives us
consolation in . . . Our sorrows and our needs . . . And He is always
willing to . . . Forgive our sinful deeds . . . And so no matter what
our wealth . . . Upon this earthly sod . . . We cannot ever pay in full
. . . The debt we owe to God.

TAKE CARE TODAY

How many cars will be destroyed . . . How many people die? . . .
As we begin to celebrate . . . The fourth day of July? . . . Why do
we get so careless when . . . A holiday draws near? . . . Why do we
turn away from God . . . And have so little fear? . . . This day is
more important than . . . We ever stop to think . . . As all our future
may be lost . . . With just a little wink . . . There may be no tomorrow if . . . We do not care today . . . And in the path of tragedy
. . . We look the other way . . . Let us be sensible this once . . .
And through this short vacation . . . Preserve the lives we need so
much . . . To carry on our nation.

AS YOU WERE BORN

Your birthday means much more to me . . . Than my own life on
earth . . . As every day I thank our God . . . That you were given
birth . . . Without the miracle that brought . . . Your heart and soul
to life . . . I never could have found myself . . . So wonderful a wife
. . . So wonderful a mother to . . . The children that are ours . . .
With loving care more beautiful . . . Than all the brightest flowers
. . . Your patience and your sacrifice . . . Deserve a world of praise
. . . And, oh, I love you, sweetheart, in . . . A thousand other ways
. . . A happy birthday, darling, and . . . Sincerely I renew . . . The
sacred promise that I made . . . To be forever true.

JUST HAVING YOU

Life is worth while for me because . . . I am in love with you . . .
And, dearest, even more because . . . I know that you are true . . .
Each day is gay with sunshine bright . . . Regardless of the weather
. . . The sunshine that is in my heart . . . As we are bound together
. . . There is no night without a moon . . . Or twinkling stars
above . . . While we are in each other's arms . . . And we remain in
love . . . There is no greatness and no praise . . . To which I could
aspire . . . Your faith in me, your loyal kiss . . . Are all that I desire
. . . Your counsel good, your patience, and . . . Your sweet and loving smile . . . Are all I ever really need . . . To make this life worth
while.

SPECIAL INTERVIEW

If your appointment book allows . . . I wish to call on you . . . To
have a most important and . . . Real special interview . . . I want to
ask some questions on . . . The confidential side . . . Provided you
will tell the truth . . . And nothing try to hide . . . I want to ask you
if you think . . . That it could ever be . . . That you would take a
vow for life . . . To love and cherish me . . . If you would please accept my heart . . . However small its worth . . . And make it the
most grateful and . . . The happiest on earth . . . And, oh, I hope
your answers, dear . . . With all my questions blend . . . So that our
interview of love . . . Will never really end.

SOLID FRIENDSHIP

Friendship is intangible . . . And yet a solid thing . . . If only by a
postal card . . . Or when the phone may ring . . . It is ethereal, and
yet . . . You know that it is there . . . As friends bestow those kindnesses . . . That prove they really care . . . Not just a handshake and
a smile . . . A little gift or two . . . Or some unusual courtesy . . .
Extended unto you . . . But that important, helping hand . . . In
time of desperate need . . . That reaches out immediately . . . To do
a generous deed . . . Yes, friendship is intangible . . . And sometimes hard to hold . . . But it can be as beautiful . . . And durable
as gold.

AS CHILDREN PLAY

The whole wide world is wonderful . . . And life is really good . . .
As long as little children play . . . Around the neighborhood . . .
Because that is a likely sign . . . That peace is still on earth . . . With
time sufficient to record . . . Another baby's birth . . . As long as
sirens do not scream . . . And whistles do not blow . . . There always
is a chance in life . . . It may continue so . . . If only now we could
be sure . . . That it would stay that way . . . With never any fear of
foes . . . Tomorrow or today . . . Let us be grateful unto God . . .
For all His blessings good . . . And pray our children will be safe
. . . In every neighborhood.

OUR FLAG OF FAITH

Old Glory flies throughout the world . . . By land and air and sea
. . . To guard the freedom that is ours . . . From every enemy . . .
Our soldiers stand on distant shores . . . Our planes patrol the skies
. . . And our great ships explore the waves . . . In search of foreign
spies . . . We pledge allegiance to our flag . . . With hand and
heart sincere . . . And bind our conscience to preserve . . . The
peace we hold so dear . . . From every mast our stars and stripes
. . . Proclaim our faith and pride . . . And symbolize the victories
. . . Of those who fought and died . . . May God be always with
us, to . . . Protect our banner bright . . . And help us keep our
courage in . . . The struggle that is right.

YOUR DAUGHTER

Your daughter is much more than just . . . One kind of many girls
. . . And in her childhood she is more . . . Than just a head of
curls . . . She is a special something that . . . Is part of all your
years . . . As she keeps growing and she shares . . . In all your
smiles and tears . . . Yes, little daughters do grow up . . . And want
their way in life . . . To follow some career, or just . . . Be happy
as a wife . . . Your daughter is no different . . . From other girls
on earth . . . Except as she is able, and . . . Would like to prove
her worth . . . In any case she's lovely, and . . . Whatever she may
do . . . She will be wonderful because . . . Her heart belongs to
you.

ALWAYS NEAR YOU

When you go to church on Sunday . . . Though you know He's
everywhere . . . Don't you feel that more than ever . . . God is
really, truly there? . . . Isn't there a certain something . . . In that
solemn atmosphere . . . That inspires you to thinking . . . God is
somewhat extra near? . . . Don't you hear the angels singing . . .
When you listen to the choir . . . And don't all your good intentions . . . Rise at least a little higher? . . . Yes, of course, you have
that feeling . . . But it is not church on Sunday . . . For that's
just a time for worship . . . You would seldom take on Monday
. . . You could always be inspired . . . If you spoke to God each
day . . . And remembered every moment . . . He is never far away.

BUYING FRIENDSHIP

Can you buy friendship on this earth . . . A friendship strong and
true? . . . And if you can, do you know what . . . The cost will be
to you? . . . Yes, you can purchase friendship real . . . But not with
gifts or cash . . . With words of sweet persuasion or . . . A promise
that is rash . . . The price of friendship is your love . . . And
willingness to be . . . The same substantial kind of friend . . .
With all sincerity . . . You must be loyal to the core . . . With
every sacrifice . . . That is the cost of friendship and . . . It is the
only price . . . No one who vows he is your friend . . . Is ever
worth your while . . . If you acquire him with cash . . . Or a de-
ceitful smile.

WE CANNOT WAIT

Remember now Pearl Harbor, and . . . Remember well that date
. . . For in this age of weapons we . . . Cannot afford to wait . . .
In 1941 we still . . . Had time for preparation . . . To save our
glorious country from . . . Complete annihilation . . . But atom
bombs and hydrogen . . . Have changed all that today . . . So
that in just a little while . . . We could be wiped away . . . Let us be
ever conscious of . . . That very costly lesson . . . And be prepared
in every way . . . To put down all aggression . . . Let us be willing
now to serve . . . By land and air and sea . . . To meet and crush
the first attack . . . Of sudden treachery.

COMFORT OTHERS

If you can comfort somebody . . . With just a word or smile . . .
If you extend a helping hand . . . Your life will be worth while
. . . You need not give your money or . . . The clothes that you
can spare . . . Though some might judge you nobler by . . . The
worldly goods you share . . . Sometimes a soothing whisper or . . . A
nudge, however slight . . . Becomes the candle that dispels . . . The
darkness of the night . . . Be kind to everyone on earth . . . As much
as you can be . . . Above all else be certain that . . . You do it willingly . . . Each time you aid your fellow man . . . You will be happier
too . . . For God will know and He will give . . . A rich reward to
you.

BACKSTAIRS

Backstairs are used by garbage men . . . The milkman and the
guy . . . Who tries to sell you all the things . . . You do not want
to buy . . . They are the pathway to the clothes . . . You hang
upon the line . . . Their railings are the gossip walls . . . Where
nosy wives recline . . . The backstairs are the playground for . . .
Your children after school . . . Who have no other place for fun
. . . By special city rule . . . They are the sometime silent route
. . . To move from place to place . . . Or just a means of quick
escape . . . To hide your worried face . . . But, most important,
backstairs are . . . The steps so tried and true . . . That guide
your neighbors on their way . . . To say hello to you.

TRULY HOME

Who wants to move from place to place? . . . Who really likes to
roam? . . . What can compare with an address . . . That truly is a
home? . . . A house, however humble, with . . . A number on a
street . . . Where relatives and neighbors and . . . All other friends
may meet . . . With all the mail deposited . . . The whole long
year around . . . And daily papers carefully . . . Tossed somewhere
on the ground . . . These are the things that make a home . . . A
paradise so gay . . . From which no one should ever feel . . . The
urge to go away . . . However more attractive may . . . Seem other
spots on earth . . . The town that is the home town is . . . The
place of greatest worth.

YOU IN MY PRAYERS

I always prayed that I would meet . . . Someone as sweet as you . . . Someone who would be really kind . . . Sincere and good and true . . . And then my prayers were answered, as . . . I gazed into your eyes . . . And it was obvious that there . . . Was not the least disguise . . . And having found you, dearest one . . . I said another prayer . . . That I could take you in my arms . . . And keep you in my care . . . God granted that petition too . . . When we became as one . . . To share the wonders of this life . . . Beneath the moon and sun . . . And now each day the prayer I say . . . Is one to help me be . . . As wonderfully devoted as . . . You always are to me.

RED-LETTER DAY

Red-letter days are those on which . . . Our happy dreams come true . . . Through circumstances fortunate . . . Or something that we do . . . They are the great occasions that . . . We know of in advance . . . Or those endearing happenings . . . That come along by chance . . . A sudden raise in salary . . . The winning of a prize . . . Or else a special party planned . . . That seems to shake the skies . . . Red-letter days are wonderful . . . And as we wish for more . . . We have it in our power now . . . To multiply the score . . . If we just do our best, and love . . . Our neighbor on our way . . . Each dawn will be the starting of . . . A real red-letter day.

OCCASIONAL CARD

Each friend we make from day to day . . . Becomes another gem . . . But each one makes it harder to . . . Keep up with all of them . . . We have just so much time in which . . . To phone or write a letter . . . Still less to pay the visit that . . . Would be a whole lot better . . . Somehow we seen so busy we . . . Can hardly turn around . . . To say hello to friends of old . . . Or those quite newly found . . . And yet we should be grateful for . . . The friendships that are ours . . . And care for every petal in . . . The garden of our flowers . . . And if we cannot call on them . . . Or see them frequently . . . At least address a greeting card . . . To each occasionally.

HAPPY MOMENTS

There are those moments wonderful . . . That I may call my own
. . . But they are not the ones I live . . . When I am all alone . . .
They are the treasured moments that . . . I spend with every
friend . . . And that I wish with all my heart . . . Would never
have an end . . . And magically for evermore . . . Those moments
stay with me . . . If only on the pages of . . . My book of memory
. . . They cannot fade or melt away . . . Or ever disappear . . .
Because they hold the story of . . . Our happiness sincere . . .
Whereas there is an emptiness . . . In moments spent alone . . .
And when they leave, I'm glad that they . . . No longer are my
own.

OUR ONLY CROWN

Dear God, how often I have prayed . . . For wealth and glory
great! . . . How often I have hungered for . . . An emperor's estate! . . . What made my heart so selfish, God? . . . Why did I
always pray . . . That everything of prominence . . . And gold
would come my way? . . . When all the time I should have known
. . . The only teaching true . . . That no one can become a king
. . . Unless he follows You . . . That money does not matter and
. . . That glory soon will fade . . . And all that ever counts on
earth . . . Is that we make the grade . . . The grade of love and
charity . . . That touches all our brothers . . . So we may earn a
lasting crown . . . By doing good for others.

OUR HAPPY CANARY

We have a cute canary with . . . A voice so sweet and strong . . .
Each time we whistle just one note . . . He bursts right into song . . .
His voice is so melodious . . . That he could qualify . . . For any
operatic notes . . . However low or high . . . Which surely proves he
does not mind . . . The cage where he must stay . . . And he has no
desire to . . . Escape and fly away . . . He is particularly fond . . .
Of any competition . . . So, when he sings, our whistling stops . . .
To give him recognition . . . But, best of all, when we may feel . . .
The very least bit blue . . . His happy trills make all our world
. . . Seem wonderful and new.

YOU ARE MY MEMORY

You are my only memories . . . Now really worth my while . . .
As you have made life wonderful . . . With every word and smile
. . . All other visions of the past . . . Are almost meaningless . . .
As you have done so much, my love . . . To bring me happiness
. . . However clearly I recall . . . Each moment I have known . . .
The ones I treasure most are those . . . That are our very own . . .
The rest are unimportant, and . . . They seem to disappear . . .
As I think only of my joy . . . With you from year to year . . . I
thank you for my memories . . . So beautiful and true . . . And
for each new one that I gain . . . Each second spent with you.

PENCIL PROBLEM

My pencils pose a problem that . . . Is not exactly light . . . Because when I have need of them . . . They never are in sight . . .
However many I may buy . . . They quickly disappear . . . And I
know who the culprit is . . . My own Kristina dear . . . She uses
them for homework or . . . When answering the phone . . . And
then she casually forgets . . . That they are not her own . . . It
would not be so bad if I . . . Could find them here and there . . .
But when my daughter "borrows" them . . . They vanish into air
. . . If pencils keep on messing up . . . The budget I must meet
. . . I may be needing some of them . . . To peddle on the street.

FAMILY LIFE

Family life embraces all . . . Of value on this earth . . . Without
it there could be no world . . . Of even passing worth . . . Con-
querors and emperors . . . Can struggle to destroy . . . And try to
force their will upon . . . Each little girl and boy . . . And they
can seize those children small . . . And make them march their
way . . . But never will they celebrate . . . A real victorious day
. . . For life on earth depends upon . . . That core of unity . . .
The composition of a close . . . And happy family . . . As babies
multiply the earth . . . And parents help them grow . . . And as
it should be obvious . . . That God decreed it so.

WEAPON OF LOVE

Love is the strongest weapon to . . . Protect our way of life . . .
Because wherever love exists . . . There is no room for strife . . .
The atom bomb, the hydrogen . . . The missile into space . . .
Can easily blow up the world . . . And everything erase . . . But
if we let our hearts be filled . . . With love for everyone . . . The
most effective bullet will . . . Be fired from our gun . . . The bullet made of friendship and . . . Of sympathy and care . . . As we
would help our neighbors, and our smallest fortune share . . . Yes,
we can overcome each foe . . . All hatred and all greed . . . For
as we love, so God will help . . . And bless our every deed.

STUDYING

Studying can do so much . . . To help improve the mind . . . As
there are never limits to . . . The knowledge we can find . . . And
it need not be difficult . . . By any kind of measure . . . Indeed if
properly approached . . . It can become a pleasure . . . If only we
will go into . . . A corner of our own . . . Where we can read in
comfort and . . . Be quietly alone . . . For there the body will relax . . . And soon the mind will follow . . . And knowledge will
be easier . . . To masticate and swallow . . . And in that atmosphere we can . . . Digest our food for thought . . . As we compare
our thinking with . . . The things that we are taught.

WARM FRIENDS, COLD

A lot of friends make promises . . . As they are fond of you . . .
But there are not so many who . . . Will really see them through
. . . They all mean well, especially . . . When all the skies are bright
. . . And when it seems quite certain that . . . The stars will shine
tonight . . . But many are the shallow ones . . . Who quickly draw
away . . . When life appears uncertain, as . . . The clouds grow
ever gray . . . They are the temporary friends . . . Who put on
quite a show . . . But who will vanish quickly when . . . Your sun
is sinking low . . . Their fever grows with praise for you . . . As
you achieve renown . . . And then as you decline a bit . . . Their
temperature goes down.

I LOVE AND NEED YOU

I love You, God, for all the things . . . That You have given me
. . . My life and happiness on earth . . . And for my family . . .
I love You for my darling spouse . . . And for our children good
. . . And every ordinary day . . . In our own neighborhood . . .
For everything in every way . . . Each smile and every tear . . . As
I appreciate Your gifts . . . And I am most sincere . . . But I do
need Your help, dear God . . . To help our children grow . . . And
make them really understand . . . The things they ought to know
. . . I cannot give my utmost to . . . The problems I must face . . .
Or ever hope to persevere . . . Without Your loving grace.

CALLUSES

Calluses are always good . . . To get on hands or knees . . . They
evidence our willingness . . . To honor, serve or please . . . Calluses on honest hands . . . That toil from day to day . . . To serve
our fellow man and please . . . The boss in every way . . . Calluses
on knees that kneel . . . In true humility . . . As we ask God to
bless us each . . . And all the family . . . Some calluses are used
to fight . . . In anger and in hate . . . Unmindful of the many sins
. . . We ought to expiate . . . When used that way they demon-
strate . . . The weakness of the soul . . . While those for labor and
for prayer . . . Strive for a worthy goal.

FAMILY PICNIC

A picnic always makes you feel . . . So youthful, gay and free . . .
It is a most delightful time . . . For all the family . . . A picnic in
the country on . . . A calm and sunny day . . . With fun and
laughter all around . . . And troubles put away . . . With all the
food that you can eat . . . And then a bit to spare . . . And song
and conversation good . . . For everyone to share . . . Perhaps a
dip into a pool . . . Or just a lazy yawn . . . And then a dreamy,
restful nap . . . Until the sun is gone . . . And so to home with weary
feet . . . But hearts refreshed once more . . . Prepared to meet whatever cares . . . And problems are in store.

BEWARE COMMITMENT

How much do you commit yourself . . . By promising to do? . . .
What is your capability . . . To really follow through? . . . Are you
inclined to promises . . . You know you cannot keep? . . . Or are you
quite prepared to climb . . . The height, however steep? . . . Whichever course, it all depends . . . Upon the words you say . . . As to your
loss in struggle or . . . Your victory today . . . You may succeed or
you may not . . . But you are better off . . . If you do not commit
yourself . . . As some might laugh or scoff . . . So think a while and
do not make . . . A statement in advance . . . You may be sure,
and yet you may . . . Be taking quite a chance.

YOUR OPPORTUNITY

Some opportunities may knock . . . But they are mighty few . . .
The chance to prove what you are worth . . . Is really up to you . . .
You have to find your way in life . . . Your choice of a career . . .
And prove that you are honest and . . . Devoted and sincere . . . In-
deed those opportunities . . . That knock upon your door . . . Are
mostly those that happen from . . . Your doing more and more . . .
The harder that you strive each day . . . For health and happiness
. . . The closer God will draw you to . . . A genuine success . . . And
so your opportunity . . . Is really up to you . . . As you accept a
certain job . . . And strive to see it through.

OUR CANARY

Of course, canaries do not talk . . . And neither does our own . . .
But ours is always happy and . . . He seldom feels alone . . . And
while he does not speak, he sings . . . For all to hear and see . . .
And his delightful voice is one . . . That lives in memory . . . Especially by day or night . . . When he has competition . . . And he
gets jealous and he strives . . . For special recognition . . . The
record player or TV . . . Or darling daughter Kris . . . When her
sweet voice is singing songs . . . You would not want to miss . . .
And then our fond canary sings . . . Until he seems to burst . . .
But finally acknowledges . . . Kristina's voice comes first.

MAGIC MOONLIGHT

Moonlight is a magic song . . . That draws our hearts away . . .
From all the cold realities . . . Of life from day to day . . . Moonlight is the time to dream . . . Of love and happiness . . . The
sweetness of a sudden kiss . . . And of a fond caress . . . But it is
not the moon alone . . . When I am with you, dear . . . In every
way, from day to day . . . I really am sincere . . . The moonlight
merely seems to add . . . That soft, romantic touch . . . Which makes
me still more conscious that . . . I love you very much . . . If now
there were no moonlight and . . . No brilliant stars to see . . . You
still would be my only love . . . And all the world to me.

I BELIEVE IN PRAYER

When I wake up each morning I . . . Recite a certain prayer . . .
That God will bless my family . . . And keep them in His care
. . . And as I cook my breakfast and . . . I shower, shave and dress
. . . I spend each moment praying for . . . Their health and happiness . . . Throughout the hours of the day . . . Wherever I may go
. . . Continually I beg of God . . . His blessings to bestow . . . And
when the clock is striking time . . . To go to bed at night . . . I pray
that we may sleep in peace . . . And all will turn out right . . . My
prayers take up the greater part . . . Of time I have to spare . . . And
that is wonderful because . . . I do believe in prayer.

GOD'S CHRISTMAS DAY

May this year's Christmas be the best . . . That you have ever had
. . . With everything that you could want . . . To make you really
glad . . . With presents bright and beautiful . . . Around the Christmas tree . . . And being able to join hands . . . With all your
family . . . And may the New Year bring to you . . . The greatest of success . . . With perfect health, prosperity . . . And every
happiness . . . But, more importantly, may God . . . Bestow His
grace on you . . . To keep you safe and guard the ones . . . Who
mean so much to you . . . And may He give to all the world . . .
The peace for which we pray . . . As we adore His only Son . . .
Jesus on Christmas Day.

BITING MY NAILS

I used to bite my fingernails . . . A long, long time ago . . . And they looked really terrible . . . I never let them grow . . . Indeed I was ashamed of the . . . Appearance of my fingers . . . And to this very moment that . . . Nightmarish memory lingers . . . One day my mind resolved to let . . . My fingernails alone . . . And very soon I was amazed . . . To see how they had grown . . . And, oh, I was so proud of them . . . And what I had been doing . . . I mean the miracle that I . . . Had suddenly stopped chewing . . . And now each fingernail of mine . . . Is like a little gem . . . As I stand guard and strive to keep . . . My teeth away from them.

LIFE POLICY

A life insurance policy . . . Is good not just in death . . . But it can help the living soul . . . To gain another breath . . . It can be borrowed on for cash . . . To meet some urgent need . . . As sickness in the family . . . Or paying up a deed . . . Or it may compensate in part . . . For incapacity . . . If the insured one should sustain . . . A crippling injury . . . The value of that policy . . . Increases every year . . . As premiums are paid on time . . . To keep the record clear . . . A life insurance policy . . . Can be our daily bread . . . It is a guardian for both . . . The living and the dead.

OUR CONSTITUTION

No other document on earth . . . No other resolution . . . Could serve a higher purpose than . . . Our U. S. Constitution . . . It guarantees the freedom of . . . The body and the mind . . . With true equality to all . . . Of very class and kind . . . It's just a piece of parchment but . . . It represents a nation . . . The greatest in the world, and why . . . We have this celebration . . . Today is Constitution Day . . . Revered in history . . . As it established and ordained . . . Our true democracy . . . God bless the fathers of our land . . . Whose brilliant contribution . . . Made possible our way of life . . . The U. S. Constitution.

GOD BLESS YOUR VOW

In all my memory there is . . . No one as sweet as you . . . No
other one who did as much . . . To make my heaven blue . . .
Who gave me so much happiness . . . Throughout each night and
day . . . With comfort, inspiration and . . . In every other way . . .
I know not why you are to me . . . So loving and so sweet . . . But
I can tell you, darling, that . . . You make my life complete . . .
And I can tell you also, dear . . . I love you tenderly . . . With all
my heart and soul and mind . . . Forever faithfully . . . Believe
me, darling, I am yours . . . By every sound and sing . . . God bless
your troth that someday soon . . . You will be always mine.

OUR BEST, DEAR DON

Happy Birthday, "lawyer" Don . . . In this your senior year . . .
Congratulations, son, to you . . . And bless your Linda dear . . .
May this new year on earth become . . . The best that you have
known . . . A golden harvest from the seed . . . Of struggle you
have sown . . . Your mother and your brother and . . . Your sister
dear and I . . . Are wishing you the best of luck . . . Up to the
highest sky . . . We thank you for the many ways . . . That you
have proved to be . . . Of everlasting credit to . . . Our loving
family . . . With your sweet bride beside you as . . . Your ever-
guiding star . . . May you receive your law degree . . . And license
at the bar.

TO DO JUST THIS

There is no other thing in life . . . I want so much to do . . . As
just to be a neighbor good . . . Considerate and true . . . To serve
my every fellow man . . . With sympathy sincere . . . And help the
whole wide world to live . . . In happiness and cheer . . . I never
want to hold a grudge . . . Or chip upon my shoulder . . . May
every day add wisdom as . . . I grow a little older . . . I want to
honor God and be . . . Of real, eternal worth . . . As I may sacrifice myself . . . For others on this earth . . . If I can do this little
bit . . . I will not cry or sigh . . . But I will feel my duty done . . .
And be prepared to die.

WHEN WE APOLOGIZE

There is no loss of character . . . In lowering our eyes . . . Indeed it calls for courage true . . . When we apologize . . . Whatever wrong we may have done . . . To cause some heart to ache . . . We help to heal the wound when we . . . Acknowledge our mistake . . . Of course there are some people who . . . Refuse apologies . . . And who would still ignore us if . . . We begged them on our knees . . . But they are not our neighbors and . . . The understanding kind . . . Who will forgive and evermore . . . Erase it from the mind . . . Indeed they never could attain . . . That truly human size . . . Where they could really understand . . . Why we apologize.

SPARE TIME

Spare time can be more valuable . . . Than time we cannot spare . . . If we are eager to progress . . . And if we really care . . . We need our relaxation and . . . Our share of fun and play . . . But there may be some moments that . . . We simply while away . . . And when we stop to think of it . . . We have no real excuse . . . For letting time slip by that we . . . Could put to extra use . . . Spare time can mean more money or . . . Some generosity . . . That may promote the welfare of . . . A whole community . . . So let us be of service, and . . . Sincerely do our share . . . For family and neighbors in . . . The time that we can spare.

FAMILY TEAM

The family must be a team . . . That works and plays together . . . In every situation and . . . In fair or stormy weather . . . The problems that arise each day . . . However large or small . . . Are those that in the family . . . Belong to one and all . . . The same as every member should . . . Receive an equal measure . . . Of happiness, affection and . . . Sweet memories to treasure . . . There must be teamwork in the home . . . As close as it can be . . . Without co-operation real . . . There is no family . . . The family team is coached by God . . . Each teammate loves the other . . . Brother, sister, Captain Dad . . . And quarterbacking Mother.

TAKE A WALK

It is refreshing exercise . . . To take a little walk . . . Especially
with someone else . . . So you may have a talk . . . A stroll around
the park or just . . . Along an avenue . . . Fresh air and friendship
at your side . . . Are always good for you . . . Each step you take
may be a stride . . . That overcomes some fear . . . Or helps to
solve a problem and . . . Makes worry disappear . . . And likewise
when your mind is free . . . And you are feeling gay . . . A little
walk will do you good . . . Whatever time of day . . . Do get in
touch with somebody . . . And take a stroll together . . . It is one
medicine that will . . . Improve your mental weather.

SUNDAY CHECK-UP

Sunday is that time each week . . . To take a special rest . . . To
pray to God and contemplate . . . If we have tried our best . . .
To think back over Monday and . . . The other days in turn . . .
And weigh our faults against the good . . . That God has helped
us learn . . . It is our opportunity . . . To take an inventory . . .
And if we failed to make the grade . . . To tell Him we are sorry . . .
Sunday is our check-up time . . . On seven days gone by . . . How
well we did, how poorly, and . . . The honest answer why . . . But
even more important as . . . We go along our way . . . Is giving
thanks to God for all . . . His blessings every day.

WE LIVE ON LABOR

However brilliant human minds . . . That guide us on our way . . .
Without the hands of labor, there . . . Would be no world today
. . . For how could any bridge design . . . Or plan for aviation
. . . Mean anything without the work . . . Of actual creation? . . .
How could atomic energy . . . Be used in peace or war . . . Unless
we had the workers who . . . Deserve that final score? . . . The ones
who labor are the ones . . . Who turn on the ignition . . . And on
this day we honor them . . . For their superb transmission . . .
There are no thanks sufficient now . . . That we could ever say
. . . But may God bless them—every one . . . On this their Labor
Day.

I KNOW YOU LOVE ME

It is not just the sunshine or . . . The sweetness of your smile . . .
The season or the weather, dear . . . That makes life seem worth-
while . . . It is not constant progress and . . . Success from day to
day . . . And not because you always are . . . So marvelously gay
. . . Nor yet the letters I receive . . . From you, my dearest friend . . .
Conveying love and marking them . . . With kisses at the end . . .
The moon does not affect me, and . . . The stars are far apart . . .
Not even all the universe . . . So activates my heart . . . What makes
my life worthwhile are all . . . The things you say and do . . . Each
one of which convinces me . . . You are sincere and true.

SECRETS

There are secrets good and bad . . . Secrets small and great . . .
Secrets that conceal a crime . . . Or cloak affairs of state . . . Secrets
of a diary . . . Or of a business deal . . . Those that are just make-
believe . . . And those that are "for real" . . . Some are very foolish
ones . . . While others make good sense . . . Some are whispered to
be passed . . . Across the back yard fence . . . Secrets fill the corner-
stone . . . Where years have passed away . . . Secrets burn the conscience of . . . The one who went astray . . . Secrets make some
people glad . . . And others feel quite smart . . . Sweetest secrets
in this life . . . Are in the lover's heart.

GOOD NEWSPAPERBOY

We honor with affection and . . . With gratitude and joy . . . Each
youngster who is serving as . . . A good newspaperboy . . . Who
brings the paper to our door . . . Each dawn or afternoon . . . So
we may know what's going on . . . Or may occur real soon . . .
Who sacrifices time for play . . . And does the best he can . . . To
please us and become a real . . . Successful businessman . . . For
he is on a certain path . . . To leadership and fame . . . As countless others in that way . . . Have gained a worthy name . . . Of
course, but just occasionally . . . He makes a few mistakes . . . We
love him and we hope he will . . . Get all the best of breaks.

DO IT TODAY

How often do we say these words . . . Before we go to bed . . .
"Tomorrow is another day . . . In which to get ahead?" . . . How
often do we put aside . . . Our problems of today . . . And think
that somewhere, somehow there . . . Will be a brighter way? . . .
We try to use a future scale . . . For every pound and ounce . . .
And do not realize that today . . . Is all that really counts . . . Tomorrow is a distant time . . . And it may never be . . . As there may
come a sudden end . . . To all of history . . . So let us do the best
we can . . . In every noble way . . . And let us try to do it while
. . . Today is still today.

WHO GIVE THEIR MOST

God loves His creatures warmly for . . . The charity they do . . .
Especially the humble ones . . . Who are sincere and true . . . A
king or other person who . . . Is loaded down with gold . . . May
help the poor in many ways . . . Most joyous to behold . . . But
he can do it easily . . . For he has wealth to spare . . . While they
whose worldly goods are few . . . Must sacrifice to share . . . Of
course the wealthy person may . . . Be just as humble, too . . .
And equally sincere of heart . . . In what he tries to do . . . And,
yet, though God rewards them all . . . As they give more and more
. . . Perhaps the poorer ones achieve . . . A little higher score.

SPARE-TIME SCHOOL

It is impossible for some . . . To go to school by day . . . Because
they have to use that time . . . To earn their weekly pay . . . They
need that money for themselves . . . Or for their parents poor . . .
Or they have children of their own . . . Whose lives must be secure
. . . But there is always night school if . . . The time can be afforded
. . . With equal opportunity . . . To rise and be rewarded . . . The
high school, business college or . . . The correspondence class . . .
With lessons no more difficult . . . Than others have to pass . . .
So why not go on learning in . . . The time there is to spare? . . .
The poor or average worker could . . . Become a millionaire.

I LOVE YOU—BUT

I, too, like sentiment, but not . . . That sad variety . . . Where I
would be so lonely, dear . . . If you were gone from me . . . Some
lovers do enjoy it when . . . Their ship is swept and tossed . . . By
winds that fairly shout to them . . . That they have loved and lost
. . . They feel so sorry for themselves . . . And let it widely known
. . . How deeply now they suffer, as . . . They feel so all alone . . .
They hope to be commended for . . . The tragic part they play . . .
Declaring that their heart is stabbed . . . And life will bleed away
. . . But that is not my attitude . . . As much as I love you . . . If you
refused me finally . . . I'd look for someone new.

SAFE DEPOSIT BOX

A safe deposit box is one . . . Where we preserve such things . . .
As contracts, stocks, insurance, wills . . . And necklaces and rings
. . . It is a special, guarded place . . . For valuables we own . . .
Provided by our chosen bank . . . For us to use alone . . . And
that is good protection for . . . A very small amount . . . And we
may go there every day . . . And all our treasures count . . . But
some things we could never put . . . In our deposit box . . . And
feel secure with guards around . . . And all the special locks . . .
Our friendships, joys and memories . . . With which we would not
part . . . Deposited more safely in . . . The strong box of the heart.

STOWAWAY JIMMIE

Our Jimmie is a stowaway . . . And puts on quite a show . . . For
he can stow away more food . . . Than anyone we know . . . He
never seems to get enough . . . Of vegetables and meat . . . Of
pies and cakes and all the things . . . He likes so much to eat . . .
Of course he is a tall young man . . . Not fat, but trim and strong
. . . And evidently needs a lot . . . Of grub to get along . . . When
he was just a little boy . . . It was a constant fight . . . To have
him drink a little milk . . . And take a second bite . . . We wish
that he had eaten more . . . Each early childhood day . . . But he
is welcome now to all . . . That he can stow away.

YOU HAD YOUR REST

If your vacation was in May . . . In June or in July . . . You may
be struggling at your job . . . With now and then a sigh . . . You
may be wishing you had been . . . More patient for your rest . . .
As August and September seem . . . The months that are the best
. . . But, after all, the choice was yours . . . Unless your boss de-
creed . . . Exactly when employees each . . . Should take the rest
they need . . . In any case, there is no cause . . . For any jealousy
. . . You had a good vacation that . . . Will live in memory . . .
And that is what you bargained for . . . Whatever time of year . . .
So count your blessings gratefully . . . And face the world with cheer.

WHEN I FEEL LOW

I thank You, God, sincerely for . . . The blessings You bestow . . .
But most of all for those You give . . . When I am feeling low
. . . When I am so discouraged and . . . My heart is really sad . . .
Because I have been lazy or . . . I know I have been bad . . . You
give me new encouragement . . . You lift my tired feet . . . And
make me feel that life again . . . Is wonderful and sweet . . . Some-
times I am so lonely I . . . Am prompted to despair . . . And then
Your grace reminds me, God . . . How much You really care . . .
How loving and forgiving and . . . How good You are to me . . .
And I just want to do Your will . . . for all eternity.

SO GLAD TO KNOW YOU

You are so wonderful a friend . . . You are so good to know . . . I
wish that you and I had met . . . A long, long time ago . . . But I am
very thankful that . . . Somehow we got together . . . For you are so
considerate . . . In every kind of weather . . . Your way of life inspires me . . . And every word you say . . . Gives faith and courage
to my heart . . . And strength from day to day . . . By every standard
high and true . . . Your friendship is a treasure . . . I hope I can repay
you in . . . The best and fullest measure . . . At least you can be certain that . . . Whatever may befall . . . I will be ready to oblige . . .
At every beck and call.

I NEED YOU NEAR

I like to walk with you at night . . . Along the avenue . . . And
talk about our future and . . . The things we plan to do . . . It is
so calm and peaceful then . . . And in your company . . . I find
the inspiration, dear . . . For all I want to be . . . The fears and
doubts that filled the day . . . Are vanished from my mind . . .
And everything seems possible . . . With courage unconfined . . .
If only I could feel that way . . . When dawn is here once more
. . . And I must face reality . . . With all its tasks in store! . . .
But that is only possible . . . If you are always near . . . Which all
depends on just how soon . . . You marry me, my dear.

HOTEL ROOM ART

Paintings can be wonderful . . . And art is quite a thing . . . With
many great museums and . . . The pleasure that they bring . . .
But many times I wonder, as . . . I travel everywhere . . . Who
decorates hotel room walls . . . At which I have to stare . . . Some
pictures are of Venice or . . . Of Paris in the rain . . . Or cowboys
herding cattle on . . . A wide and flat terrain . . . I see no famous
painting or . . . A replica thereof . . . That could inspire me with
thoughts . . . Of beauty or of love . . . Hotels can be quite wonderful . . . As here and there I roam . . . But I do wish their pictures
would . . . Remind me more of home.

WILL YOU BE SANE?

There will be crazy motorists . . . The fourth day of July . . . And
many families will mourn . . . The loved ones who will die . . . It
does not have to be that way . . . And it is most unfair . . . But
always there are idiots . . . Who do not seem to care . . . The ones
who need no warning, and . . . Who never comtemplate . . . The
probability of death . . . Until it is too late . . . The same as careless swimmers and . . . The ones with mental quirks . . . Who exercise no caution as . . . They handle fireworks . . . Will you remember to have sense . . . Or go your foolish way . . . To slaughter
others or destroy . . . Yourself this holiday?

TASTE AND COMFORT

Whenever you buy any clothes . . . Be sure they fit you well . . .
For comfort is the quality . . . In which they should excel . . .
Select and try each item on . . . With patience and with care . . .
Especially when getting set . . . To travel anywhere . . . Appear-
ance is important to . . . The ones you hope to please . . . And
therefore you should look and feel . . . Entirely at ease . . . A
suit or dress too tight or loose . . . Disturbs appraising eyes . . .
The same as garb that is too loud . . . Including hose and ties . . .
And why not be particular . . . When you consider it? . . . The
cash you spend entitles you . . . To tasteful clothes that fit.

WHO FISH FOR FUN

Some occupations call for skill . . . Including many sports . . . But
anybody can become . . . A fisherman of sorts . . . If he just has a
bamboo pole . . . A certain length of string . . . A cork, a hook and
worm, then he . . . Can catch most anything . . . The only other
requisite . . . Is patience tried and true . . . To brave the sun in
silence, and . . . To wait the hours through . . . Of course he must
be satisfied . . . With average lakes and streams . . . And sailfish,
marlin and the like . . . Are far beyond his dreams . . . But still
he is a fisherman . . . And what he lacks in skill . . . Is more than
compensated for . . . By his vacation thrill.

YOUR GOLD STAR FLAG

How many gold stars do you have . . . Upon your flag today . . .
Reflecting kindly thoughts and words . . . And deeds along your way?
. . . The stars of courtesy and tact . . . And tolerance to all . . . Sincere forgiveness and the smiles . . . That weave a gentle shawl . . .
The star of deep humility . . . And that of friendship true . . . With
no desire to obtain . . . The least reward for you . . . What sacrifices
do you make? . . . What comfort do you give . . . To friend and
stranger striving for . . . A better way to live? . . . God scores the gold
stars on your flag . . . With interest compound . . . But only if you
do not hoist . . . And wave your flag around.

IT'S WONDERFUL

It's wonderful to be in love . . . It's wonderful to know . . . That you return my feelings, and . . . You really love me so . . . It's wonderful to hold you in . . . My arms when stars are bright . . . And touch my lips to yours, dear one . . . To say a sweet good night . . . To wake up in the morning by . . . The tingling of the phone . . . And be reminded by your voice . . . That you are mine alone . . . It's wonderful to be assured . . . By mail and telegram . . . Your true and only sweetheart is . . . The one you say I am . . . Each moment at your side becomes . . . A treasured memory . . . It's wonderful you really are . . . So much in love with me.

REJOICE IN JESUS

Let us rejoice in Jesus on . . . This wondrous Easter Day . . . And with humility of heart . . . Be grateful as we pray . . . Thank God that His beloved Son . . . Has risen from the grave . . . Who gave us His example to . . . Be virtuous and brave . . . All glory be to Him this day . . . All praise and music sweet . . . As we adore our Lord and God . . . And worship at His feet . . . And may this Easter bless us with . . . The inspiration true . . . To honor God, and serve him well . . . With everything we do . . . Let us resolve this Easter Day . . . To make another start . . . And promise to put forth our best . . . With soul and mind and heart.

OBEY AT HOME

Obedience at home is not . . . Intended just to please . . . The parents who require it . . . Or simply to appease . . . It is not for their benefit . . . But for the children's good . . . So they will grow in character . . . As everybody should . . . It helps them reach their future goal . . . Whatever it may be . . . By teaching them the value of . . . Dependability . . . For they will not be able to . . . Command their own someday . . . Unless in youth they are prepared . . . And willing to obey . . . As children give allegiance to . . . Their fathers and their mothers . . . So they will gain the loyalty . . . And the respect of others.

THE GOOD OF WAR

Nobody wants, and we all dread . . . The very thought of war . . .
And yet when battle rages, we . . . Accomplish so much more . . .
It suddenly reminds us of . . . Our precious liberty . . . We grow
more patriotic, and . . . We have more sympathy . . . We go all out
to help produce . . . The guns and food we need . . . We purchase
bonds, and give our blood . . . For men who fall and bleed . . . We
comfort Gold Star mothers, and . . . Do everything we can . . . With
labor and with charity . . . To help each fellow man . . . Sometimes
it seems it has to be . . . That God allows a war . . . To draw our
hearts to Him, and to . . . Accomplish so much more.

YOU OWE YOUR BOSS

The office is no place to nap . . . Not even when you're through . . .
With each and every duty which . . . Has been assigned to you . . .
For you agreed upon a length . . . Of service day to day . . . And
your employer promised you . . . A stipulated pay . . . And therefore if your work is done . . . Before it's time to quit . . . You should
approach him instantly . . . And you should tell him it . . . The obligation of your job . . . Is just as much your own . . . When your
employer is at hand . . . As when you are alone . . . And you will be
much better off . . . Without that "stolen" rest . . . As every boss
appreciates . . . The one who serves him best.

SLOPPY GIRLS

A teen-age girl is sloppy with . . . Her bedroom and her clothes . . .
Her schoolbooks, homework, everything . . . As every parent knows
. . . Our darling daughter Kris is no . . . Exception to the rule . . .
Nor Lynn and Carol who are quite . . . Her special friends in school
. . . Their dresses and their shoes and socks . . . They toss around and
leave . . . For mother or perhaps a maid . . . To search for and re-
trieve . . . Dear mother tries to teach them but . . . They never seem
to learn . . . Their sloppiness is not to them . . . Of any great concern . . . But when they have their children it . . . Will be a different
story . . . And as they'll long for neatness then . . . They surely will
be sorry.

IN ALL THE WORLD

I could walk up and down every street in our town . . . And know that I never would see . . . Someone else on this earth of such marvelous worth . . . As you are forever to me . . . I could stroll every lane in the sun and the rain . . . Or the forests so deep and so high . . . And look everywhere, with the greatest of care . . . In the cities that reach to the sky . . . But nobody else could ever bestow . . . Your softly embracing touch . . . And never another could I find . . . To love and to cherish so much . . . I could wander the world, with its oceans wide . . . To the farthest and strangest ports . . . From the lowliest street of forgotten feet . . . To the most exotic resorts . . . I could follow the path of the moon and the stars . . . And search for the smallest clue . . . And never discover another soul . . . As charming and sweet as you.

FREEDOM FOREVER

Although our wars have left their scars . . . As we have fought our way . . . We still are free to celebrate . . . Our Independence Day . . . Our stripes are still the colonies . . . Our stars reflect the states . . . That tolerate no tyranny . . . And have no use for hates . . . Our nation is united in . . . The cause for freedom true . . . As much as human liberty . . . Is dear to me and you . . . And so Old Glory waves today . . . And we are glad and proud . . . And we have every right to march . . . And sing our praise out loud . . . And as we pause our labor now . . . To celebrate this day . . . We hope our polls will always keep . . . Our democratic way.

HOME LIBRARY

Some people build home libraries . . . With books they have not read . . . And which, they think, they have no time . . . To even read in bed . . . But, oh, they want those volumes, and . . . They say the day will come . . . When they will study all of them . . . Or quite a few, or some . . . Someday when they retire, and . . . Have nothing else to do . . . Than just to chose a famous work . . . And pore the pages through . . . But ironclad intentions can . . . Get covered up with rust . . . And many are the shelves of books . . . That merely gather dust . . . The best library in the home . . . Is built up now and then . . . With treasured tomes that have been read . . . And will be read again.

THE MIND MUST GUIDE

There are so many instruments . . . With which to write today . . .
It should be easy to put down . . . The words we want to say . . .
There are so many pencils now . . . Mechanical and plain . . . With
common black or colored lead . . . To help the hand and brain . . .
And there are pens of every style . . . And size that we may find . . .
The fountain and the ball point and . . . The cartridge loading kind
. . . Yes, they are very useful with . . . Their ready lead or ink . . .
But they cannot form sentences . . . Or help the head to think . . .
The mind must first instruct the hand . . . That moves the instrument
. . . Before a word can be composed . . . Or any message sent.

CREDITS AND GRADES

In high school days some years ago . . . Each credit that was gained
. . . Was prima facie evidence . . . Of knowledge well attained . . .
No matter what the grade we made . . . "Just passing" or the best
. . . Each credit that was certified . . . Was good as all the rest . . .
And so it was not difficult . . . To qualify for college . . . Regardless
of capacity . . . To really grow in knowledge . . . But college population growth . . . Has raised the standards so . . . That credits do
not certify . . . How much or well we know . . . Our actual grades
are weighed, and then . . . Some schools require, too . . . A test to
prove we are prepared . . . To meet horizons new.

A FEW ARE TRUE

We have so many friendships that . . . Remind us of the past . . .
And friendships make us happy but . . . How many of them last?
. . . How many of them linger for . . . A season or a year? . . . How
many last still longer now . . . Or quickly disappear? . . . Oh, there
are friends who promise us . . . That they will never fail . . . Not
even if we make mistakes . . . And have to go to jail . . . And usually
they are the ones . . . From whom we never hear . . . Until our
worries reach their end . . . And we are in the clear . . . But, by the
grace of God, there are . . . Some friendships that begin . . . And
stay with us through every storm . . . However thick or thin.

IF YOU WANT ME

The reason I have never said . . . How much I think of you . . . Is just because your heart might doubt . . . My sentiments are true . . . And you may still be doubtful that . . . You mean so much to me . . . In every dream of days to come . . . And every memory . . . I have been very much afraid . . . And so I am today . . . That you might smile politely, dear . . . Then turn your head away . . . But now I want to take the chance . . . And truthfully declare . . . You are the only one with whom . . . This life I want to share . . . Accept me or refuse me, dear . . . As you decide to do . . . However you may feel, my heart . . . Will still belong to you.

SINCERE ON SUNDAY

So often after church—as soon . . . As we are once outside . . . We lose our brief humility . . . And we regain our pride . . . Our prayers are all forgotten and . . . Our good intentions too . . . The wrongs to be forgiven, and . . . Those friendships to renew . . . The gossip that we promised we . . . Would never spread again . . . As we recall some rumor that . . . We whispered there and then . . . What good is any Sunday church . . . When always in between . . . We prove to God our promises . . . We do not really mean? . . . Why occupy God's time in church? . . . Why bother to appear . . . If worship is a pretense, and . . . The heart is not sincere?

LIKE FATHER, LIKE SON

A father wants his son to think . . . He is the grandest guy . . . Who can accomplish anything . . . That he sets out to try . . . Who is so wise in every way . . . And always good and kind . . . With welfare of the family . . . Especially in mind . . . And that is only natural . . . For as his son thinks . . . That pattern will inspire him . . . Wherever he may go . . . And he, in turn, will want his son . . . To think the very same . . . As one more generation strives . . . To bear a worthy name . . . But doing this takes more than just . . . A wishful fantasy . . . The father must be nearly all . . . Of what he seems to be.

YOUR KEY TO HEAVEN

If there is anything to gain . . . From riches in this life . . . It is to do your part to ease . . . The struggle and the strife . . . To help your neighbor and your friend . . . In moments of distress . . . And give to every worthy cause . . . A share of your success . . . God does not love the miser who . . . Would hide upon his shelf . . . The wealth beyond his needs that he . . . Has gathered to himself . . . Be not the foolish camel that . . . Would pierce the needle's eye . . . But do some good upon this earth . . . Before the day you die . . . Be generous within your means . . . And then a little more . . . And in return you will receive . . . Your key to Heaven's door.

TRAVELING WEST

If, traveling west, you tire of . . . The mountains, plains and skies . . . Then you are looking at the world . . . With undiscerning eyes . . . You do not see the beauty of . . . The wonders God designed . . . Beyond all power to conceive . . . By any human mind . . . You do not sense the majesty . . . Of heaven and of earth . . . The glory of the Golden West . . . The miracle of birth . . . Nor do you feel the peace that seems . . . To sanctify the soul . . . Alone with God in fairyland . . . Where life is sweet and whole . . . But look again and think again . . . And maybe you will see . . . This awe-inspiring mirage . . . Of God's eternity.

SLEEPY WEATHER

Although I do my work at night . . . And sleep throughout the day . . . The weather is important, as . . . The forecasts come my way . . . According to the news in print . . . TV and radio . . . I try to keep myself informed . . . On how the wind may blow . . . Because there are those problems when . . . I crawl into my bed . . . If I should turn the covers down . . . Or pull them on my head . . . If I should close the window, to . . . Avoid the rain or sleet . . . Or shut the blinds against the sun . . . With light and added heat . . . For those who work all day, I hope . . . The weather will be fair . . . As for myself, I want to know . . . Which PJs I should wear.

TO WIN OVER SIN

I thank you, God, for everything . . . Each blessing day and night
. . . Especially the grace to do . . . The things I know are right . . . I
may not always do them, God . . . As You are well aware . . . And
sometimes I feel lost and I . . . Am given to despair . . . I know it is
so wrong for me . . . To have that kind of mood . . . And that the
weakness of my flesh . . . Reflects ingratitude . . . My heart is truly
sorry, God . . . Sincerely I repent . . . And beg for more abundant
grace . . . As virtue's battlement . . . Please comfort me and heal each
wound . . . That I sustain from sin . . . Then lift me up once more,
dear God . . . With strength enough to win.

LEAP YEAR DAY

Each fourth year is a Leap Year and . . . Today is Leap Year Day
. . . When every girl may grab a boy . . . And spirit him away . . .
When it is perfect etiquette . . . For ladies to disclose . . . That they
adore a certain man . . . And daringly propose . . . And yet it is a
silly and . . . Unnecessary thing . . . Because their lasso is the same
. . . As any wedding ring . . . The other three years out of four
. . . They do it just as much . . . Except, of course, that they em-
ploy . . . A somewhat subtle touch . . . The only difference is that
when . . . There is a Leap Year new . . . The female of the species
may . . . Quite openly pursue.

FRIENDSHIP GERM

Friendship can be catching as . . . A wonderful disease . . . And you
can help to spread it if . . . You do your best to please . . . Friendship will not make you ill . . . But ever so much glad . . . And rouse
you from your doldrums when . . . You think that you are sad . . .
Meet some person, say hello . . . And simply shake a hand . . . And
as you see a friendly smile . . . Your heart will understand . . .
Friendship is contagious as . . . The germ that gives a cold . . . But
all that it afflicts you with . . . Is love and joy to hold . . . So try to
be contagious in . . . Your contacts every day . . . By shaking hands
and smiling as . . . You go along your way.

DO NOT DESPAIR

Whatever miseries you have . . . However sad you are . . . You still can say a prayer to God . . . And wish upon a star . . . You may be desperate, and feel . . . Your life has reached its end . . . And you may even think that you . . . Have not a single friend . . . And yet there always is a chance . . . That life will turn out good . . . As you still have your family . . . And all your neighborhood . . . They are your fellow humans, and . . . They really care for you . . . And if you let them, they will try . . . To prove that they are true . . . So don't give up, and don't despair . . . But try it one more day . . . Remember God is at your side . . . To help you on your way.

AS WE ARE NEIGHBORS

The problems of a home are not . . . As many as we think . . . Including all the dusting and . . . The dishes in the sink . . . Yes, there are beds that should be made . . . And meals we must prepare . . . And sometimes there are little tears . . . That need our special care . . . There is the laundry to be done . . . The buttons to be sewed . . . And all the monthly bills that seem . . . To multiply our load . . . But we are not a bankrupt firm . . . We are a family . . . And we believe in God and in . . . Our great democracy . . . And always there are neighbors who . . . Are more than glad to share . . . Their comfort and their happiness . . . To show how much they care.

PASS IT ON

A certain father helped his son . . . Begin his life's career . . . Financially and with advice . . . To overcome his fear . . . The son was grateful, and he said . . . Someday he would repay . . . Twice the amount that he received . . . To start him on his way . . . "Dear son, I do not want it back" . . . His father told him then . . . "Just pass it on to someone else . . . To do some good again" . . . His was the kindly attitude . . . Each of us should possess . . . To do the best and most we can . . . For human happiness . . . We should not seek repayment or . . . Reward for brain or brawn . . . But just request the one we helped . . . Someday to pass it on.

GOD GIVE ME YOU

I never let you know before . . . But now I must confess . . . That
only in your loving arms . . . Could I find happiness . . . Yes, it has
taken quite a while . . . To tell you how I feel . . . But I just wanted
to be sure . . . My love for you was real . . . And now I realize, darling, that . . . No other one would do . . . As no one else could mean
so much . . . And I want only you . . . Perhaps I lingered overtime
. . . And I may be too late . . . You may have chosen someone else
. . . More suited to your taste . . . But if I still have any chance . . .
For what I hope will be . . . May God perform the miracle . . . Of
giving you to me.

KRIS NEEDS NO CASH

Kristina never asks me for . . . The least amount of cash . . . She does
not yearn for money, and . . . Her ways are never brash . . . Regardless of the greenbacks or . . . The coins I have on hand . . . She
does not ever bother me . . . By making some demand . . . For Kris,
my daughter, sweet fourteen . . . Is quite a diplomat . . . And she
knows well how she can put . . . A feather in her hat . . . She simply
lets me know she wants . . . A certain thing or two . . . And so she
gets them every time . . . What else can Daddy do? . . . She does
not want cold cash to spend . . . But only that I buy . . . Such large
or little luxuries . . . As may attract her eye.

DO A FAVOR

Do a friend a favor and . . . He does one in return . . . If he is that
devoted kind . . . For which all humans yearn . . . His thank-you
favor need not be . . . Of monetary worth . . . It could be much more
valuable . . . Than all the wealth on earth . . . By just his pleasant
company . . . His smile and conversation . . . That makes you feel
almost as though . . . He were a blood relation . . . Favors are not
money spent . . . Except as they may be . . . The sort of help most
needed in . . . A real emergency . . . Do a favor for a friend . . .
And be a friend to all . . . You'll be surprised how most will be . . .
Right at your beck and call.

IF YOU LOVE ME

With all my love I come to you . . . I offer you my heart . . . And
promise you most faithfully . . . That we will never part . . . I mean
that we shall never part . . . Unless you go away . . . For I cannot
control your mind . . . And tell you what to say . . . But if you feel
the way I do . . . And give your heart to me . . . Our life will be a
paradise . . . For all eternity . . . Because I know I love you and
. . . There is no other one . . . Who is as wonderful to me . . . Beneath the moon or sun . . . And so if you have faith in me . . . As
I believe in you . . . Our future will be rosy and . . . Our dreams will
all come true.

WE BELONG TO GOD

As God created everything . . . So we belong to Him . . . With all
our joys and sorrows and . . . Our hopes, however dim . . . Our
dreams and our ambitions and . . . Our charity or greed . . . As we
may live from day to day . . . By thought and word and deed . . . No
victory belongs to us . . . No talent is our own . . . Though sometimes God allows some praise . . . For efforts we have shown . . . He
lets us go along our path . . . The best way that we can . . . And
hopes that we will honor Him . . . And serve our fellow man . . .
But whether we would rule the world . . . Or just the surface skim
. . . Our bodies and our souls and minds . . . Belong at last to Him.

BOARD CHAIRMAN

Sometimes the Chairman of the Board . . . Is quite a man of power
. . . And there are times when he can be . . . The hero of the hour
. . . But not infrequently he is . . . A gentleman retired . . . Whose
service to the company . . . Has more or less expired . . . There are
no burdens great or small . . . That he is forced to carry . . . Indeed
his title actually . . . Amounts to "honorary" . . . Of course he
shows that natural pride . . . At luncheon or at dinner . . . In private
clubs where he still hopes . . . To stand out as a winner . . . There
is the Chairman of the Board . . . Who serves his firm and nation
. . . And one who just relaxes and . . . Enjoys his reputation.

LET'S HURRY SLOWLY

It's good to be ambitious but . . . We should be patient, too . . . In order to accomplish what . . . We really want to do . . . We can get so excited that . . . We spoil our steady aim . . . And also we may find ourselves . . . A little limp and lame . . . There is that old expression true . . . That sometimes haste makes waste . . . And to that human error now . . . Some tragedies are traced . . . There is no sense in rushing in . . . "Where angels fear to tread" . . . When just a little common sense . . . May help us get ahead . . . So let us mix ambition with . . . The patience we require . . . Before we strike the match we think . . . Will set the world on fire.

OUR AFRICAN VELDT

In Africa wild animals . . . Are not inclined to mix . . . And birds are always wary of . . . Each other's deadly tricks . . . But they all thrive together in . . . Our Kansas City Zoo . . . The Sarus crane and Demoiselle . . . The elephant and gnu . . . The zebra and the eland and . . . The ostrich and giraffe . . . And others that entrance us or . . . Provoke a gentle laugh . . . For in our zoo there is a veldt . . . As native as can be . . . Where kindly care induces them . . . To live in harmony . . . It is indeed a marvel of . . . Our present age and day . . . Wild Africa converted to . . . Our democratic way.

SLEEPY PRETZEL

One thing that sort of fascinates . . . Yet always puzzles me . . . Is how a dog can close his eyes . . . And slumber constantly . . . Our dachshund, Pretzel, illustrates . . . That very lazy sight . . . He snores his head off through the day . . . And then he sleeps all night . . . Of course he has to eat and drink . . . And he runs out to play . . . But we can count the minutes he . . . Is actually away . . . And half of every little while . . . Our Pretzel may be gone . . . He seems to spend luxuriously . . . Stretched out upon the lawn . . . We do not mind his dozing, for . . . He is our precious pet . . . But when it comes to idleness . . . How lazy can he get?

WHY SECRETS, LOVE?

There are so many differences . . . That you and I divide . . . So
many things I keep from you . . . And those you try to hide . . . If
only I could tell you all . . . The secrets in my heart . . . I do believe sincerely now . . . That we would never part . . . And yet I do
not know, my love . . . The secrets that you keep . . . The ones when
we are wide awake . . . Or when we are asleep . . . Why do we hold
these secrets from . . . Each other anyway . . . When we must meet
and we must be . . . Together every day? . . . Whatever secrets you
may have . . . I whisper mine to you . . . To let you know I love you
and . . . I always have been true.

GOD, MAKE HIM WELL

Dear God, I know my failures and . . . How little I am worth . . .
But I do ask that You perform . . . This miracle on earth . . . This
miracle for someone who . . . Would live a little longer . . . And
who could not, without Your help . . . Become the least bit stronger
. . . For someone who would serve You, God . . . With heart sincere
and true . . . And who would be forever glad . . . And grateful unto
You . . . Who is so ill—who needs Your hand . . . Or breath, however lightly . . . To put away his ailments and . . . His troubles so
unsightly . . . Yes, he has sinned, as all of us . . . Transgress along
our way . . . But please forgive him, God, and grant . . . This miracle
today.

A SINGLE FRIEND

As long as I am fortunate . . . To have a single friend . . . I shall not
feel alone in life . . . Unto its very end . . . A gentle friend who is
sincere . . . And who is always true . . . Who helps me in a kindred
way . . . To see my struggles through . . . One friend forever at my
side . . . When others drift away . . . With hand and heart available
. . . Each moment, night and day . . . I treasure all the friends I
have . . . Yet one is quite enough . . . When skies are ominous and
when . . . The going gets real rough . . . And I shall praise and
pray for him . . . Or her, as it may be . . . Who will defend me to the
last . . . With faith and loyalty.

147

LET'S NOT ARGUE

Whenever we two argue, and . . . I walk away from you . . . My dearest, please forgive me for . . . Whatever I may do . . . I do not mean to hurt you, love . . . With anything I say . . . I only want to wake you up . . . To live a wiser way . . . The only reason, darling, that . . . I wander from your side . . . Is that I hope you will regret . . . And overcome your pride . . . I know sometimes the fault is mine . . . Sometimes you are to blame . . . In any case, we both are wrong . . . And it is quite a shame . . . And so as you embrace me, and . . . I cherish you, my dear . . . Let us reduce our arguments . . . Until they disappear.

AS SCHOOL BEGINS

School begins today for those . . . Who want an education . . . And who are really interested . . . In furthering our nation . . . School begins for boys and girls . . . In their initial grade . . . And everyone this time of year . . . Who seeks scholastic braid . . . The student in the high school, and . . . The one who is in college . . . Intent upon acquiring . . . A wealth of greater knowledge . . . School is education, and . . . The most important part . . . Of lifting us above the crowd . . . And giving us a start . . . Let us be glad that school once more . . . Is happily beginning . . . As it informs us and promotes . . . The chances of our winning.

CAN'T STAND KIDS?

Do neighbors' children bother you . . . When you are all alone? . . . Most likely it is true, unless . . . You have some of your own . . . If now you are a bachelor . . . A widow or old maid . . . You may resent those noises when . . . Young Indians make a raid . . . You may not like those tricycles . . . That cut across your lawn . . . Or shouts that greet another day . . . When it is barely dawn . . . But stop and think that babies keep . . . Our hopes and dreams alive . . . And only as they follow us . . . Can all the world survive . . . And if by God's good grace you had . . . Some children of your own . . . You would not mind their racket, and . . . You would not feel alone.

LISTEN, DARLING

Listen to me, darling, now . . . Please believe me, dear . . . Every whisper of my vow . . . Is honest and sincere . . . Please believe that I am true . . . And you will not be sorry . . . What I want to say to you . . . Is not a fairy story . . . No one else could mean so much . . . In every way to me . . . Or even have that perfect touch . . . Of love and sympathy . . . Please believe me when I say . . . My heart is yours forever . . . And I will never go away . . . Today, tomorrow—never . . . Listen and believe me, dear . . . Whatever moon or sun . . . My promise, dear, is most sincere . . . You are the only one.

I BELIEVE IN GOD

If I grow weary in my heart . . . Along the way I plod . . . I do not fear, because I know . . . It is the will of God . . . I know that each misfortune is . . . His way of trying me . . . And only as I bow to Him . . . Shall I have victory . . . Without His grace I could not live . . . I could not breathe the air . . . I could not do a single thing . . . Without His loving care . . . And that is why I pray to God . . . Each morning and each night . . . However happy I may be . . . Or sorry is my plight . . . And that is why I never fear . . . When skies grow dark or dim . . . My God is watching over me . . . And I have faith in Him.

MAIL CARRIER

The man who brings the mail to us . . . Has quite a job to do . . . Considering the strain and stress . . . He constantly goes through . . . Of course the first and foremost is . . . The weather of the day . . . As snow and sleet or rain or heat . . . May slow him on his way . . . And then there are the untrained dogs . . . That bark and nip or bite . . . And those inhuman humans who . . . Are always impolite . . . He has to have both brawn and brain . . . Especially the latter . . . For he must be familiar with . . . Most every postal matter . . . His task would be much lighter as . . . He goes from door to door . . . If only everybody would . . . Appreciate him more.

WHICH WAY IN LIFE?

I wander on the beach at dawn . . . And I behold the sea . . . And
every wave that touches shore . . . Becomes a reverie . . . I see the
sails of long ago . . . Majestic in the sun . . . The men-of-war returning from . . . Decisive battles won . . . And then I see the derelicts
. . . Like ghost ships in the night . . . Of lurid fascination but . . .
A bootless ocean blight . . . Which of these two, I ask myself . . .
Will I become some day . . . The hollow hull adrift at sea . . . Or
flagship in the bay? . . . Have I the courage and the strength . . . To
conquer storm and strife? . . . Or have I not the backbone now . . .
To live a useful life?

GIVE ALL YOU CAN

This is the annual appeal . . . For all to do their best . . . To help the
whole community . . . By filling up the Chest . . . This is that inventory time . . . To count your blessings good . . . As God has favored
you at work . . . And in your neighborhood . . . And so decide the
certain sum . . . You can afford to give . . . To help the ones who
need your help . . . Wherever you may live . . . No one will ask or
wonder if . . . You tried to do your part . . . For charity is up to you
. . . According to your heart . . . Just God will weigh the value of
. . . The sacrifice you make . . . And count your offering as one . . .
For His beloved sake.

THE HELPING HAND

The other day I visited . . . A friend of long ago . . . Who helped
me learn so many things . . . That I have come to know . . . And it
was really wonderful . . . To talk with him and roam . . . Around the
charming premises . . . That now he calls his home . . . And there I
saw the painting that . . . Is named "The Helping Hand" . . . A fisherman and little girl . . . Who made me understand . . . That nothing is more wonderful . . . Than just to have a friend . . . The kind
that really trusts in you . . . Today and to the end . . . The same as
in that painting where . . . The small girl grips the oar . . . To help
the kindly fisherman . . . Get safely back to shore.

LET'S BE FRIENDS?

What can I say when I behold . . . The hurt look in your eyes . . .
Except that I am sorry, dear? . . . I do apologize . . . I mean it, dear,
with all my heart . . . I want to make amends . . . Forgive me now,
and let us be . . . The same good, happy friends . . . Let us forget
it happened, dear . . . And how and where and when . . . I firmly
promise not to make . . . The same mistake again . . . These are the
only thoughts and words . . . That I can offer you . . . Believe me,
dear, my feelings and . . . These sentiments are true . . . Whatever
I have wanted, dear . . . Has been for your own sake . . . Please,
let it not be all in vain . . . Because of one mistake.

NO TASK IMPOSSIBLE

There is no task impossible . . . If we believe and pray . . . And if
we really try to do . . . Our best in every way . . . Our faith in God
and in ourselves . . . With hope and fervent prayer . . . And in the
knowledge spiritual . . . That God is always there . . . These are the
tools and weapons that . . . We need to make the grade . . . These
are the substances of which . . . All miracles are made . . . Our
shoulder must be at the wheel . . . With persevering might . . . And
more important than all else . . . Our thinking must be right . . .
Faith and hope and work and prayer . . . Are bound to bring success
. . . And gain the greatest goal of all—. . . Eternal happiness.

SAFER BY DAYLIGHT

I never like to drive at night . . . It always frightens me . . . Unless I
have no choice because . . . Of some emergency . . . The shadows
flicker all around . . . The passing headlights glare . . . And I thank
God for journey's end . . . When I am safely there . . . In younger
days behind the wheel . . . I did not mind the night . . . I thought
it was adventure and . . . It gave me much delight . . . But I have
learned that driving is . . . More dangerous in the dark . . . And
there are greater hazards when . . . We take the time to park . . . In
daylight it is easier . . . For anyone to drive . . . And so much better
are the odds . . . For us to stay alive.

DEDICATED MAN

A dedicated man is one . . . Who helps a worthy cause . . . Without expecting in return . . . Great praise or loud applause . . . He gives his efforts day and night . . . As much as he can spare . . . To serve his own community . . . And people everywhere . . . He never tires of that task . . . But he goes on and on . . . To aid his fellow man and bring . . . The world a brighter dawn . . . A dedicated man is one . . . Whose heart is so sincere . . . He feels no matter what may be . . . He has to persevere . . . If only there were more of him . . . Upon this earth today . . . The path we have to plod would be . . . A less exhausting way.

I. Q. TEST

An I.Q. test may indicate . . . That you are very smart . . . But that is no assurance you . . . Will play a brilliant part . . . For it is not how bright you are . . . That scores success for you . . . But how you live from day to day . . . And what you really do . . . You may be quite ingenious . . . And yet what does it mean . . . Unless you use that gift from God . . . To help the human scene? . . . You could devote your talents to . . . A life of shame and crime . . . Or you could just ignore the world . . . And while away your time . . . No I.Q. rating ever is . . . True cause for pride or praise . . . Your laurels on this earth depend . . . On your unselfish ways.

LEARNING AT NIGHT

The public night school is for those . . . Who want to get ahead . . . By utilizing leisure time . . . Before they go to bed . . . It is for young and old alike . . . And close to being free . . . As usually the only cost . . . Is just a token fee . . . The public night school is for those . . . Who work throughout the day . . . Or those with idle hours they . . . Prefer to spend that way . . . Or married folks who otherwise . . . Could not go out at night . . . Because they sensibly agree . . . Their budget is too tight . . . So whether just to pass the time . . . Or graduate from college . . . The public night school offers all . . . The chance to grow in knowledge.

SO TRUE TO ME

I remember the night when the sky was bright . . . With a golden
moon above . . . And the silvery stars surrounded us . . . In our wonderful world of love . . . I remember the breeze that caressed the trees
. . . On the path to your garden gate . . . Where I kissed your lips
and you promised me . . . Forever and ever to wait . . . Whichever
the road, whatever the load . . . Wherever my steps might go . . .
Your heart would never be shaken by . . . The treacherous winds
that blow . . . And the years went by, and at last the sky . . . Was
gorgeous as it was then . . . And by the wonderful grace of God . . .
I gazed in your eyes again . . . God bless you, love, for the hope in my
heart . . . And never will I forget . . . Your faith in me and your loyalty . . . From the marvelous moment we met.

OUR WORTHY ALL

One God, one flag, one family . . . These are our all on earth . . .
And only as we honor them . . . Are we of any worth . . . Our faith
in God with fervent prayer . . . Our patriotic score . . . Of loyalty
to government . . . In time of peace and war . . . Devotion to our
spouse and to . . . The children whom we rear . . . Preserving honor,
guarding all . . . Good things we hold so dear . . . What else is there
to live for if . . . We ever hope to be . . . Rewarded for our mortal
span . . . In God's eternity? . . . What gain is there in selfishness
. . . Cupidity or pride . . . That bind the bridegroom, Satan, and
Eternal Death, his bride?

OLD FOLKS AT HOME

Our eldest son is married and . . . Is living far away . . . And now
the younger son real soon . . . Will have his wedding day . . . Our
darling daughter's bags are packed . . . And she can hardly wait . . .
To get back to her school and friends . . . In quite a distant state
. . . And so it seems apparent that . . . As our dear children roam
. . . My loving wife and I will be . . . The only ones at home . . .
Yes, we are getting older and . . . We shall be all alone . . . But we
will not be lonely—thanks . . . To mail and telephone . . . Yes, we
will miss them very much . . . Yet we will not be sad . . . Because
we want their hearts to be . . . In every way real glad.

OLD MEMORIES

There are those special memories . . . We cherish through the years
. . . The most of them are happy ones . . . A few are touched by
tears . . . They all become more beautiful . . . The older now they
grow . . . And with their age they take their place . . . As days of
long ago . . . They are the pictures of a past . . . For which we
sometimes yearn . . . But which we know so well is gone . . . And
which cannot return . . . They have no market value in . . . Our com-
merce of today . . . They are not even anything . . . That we can
give away . . . And yet those memories can play . . . A most important part . . . As they inspire or console . . . Or elsewise help the
heart.

LOVELORN

The lovelorn are the ones who weep . . . With never any pride . . .
Who feel their fortune was unfair . . . When they were cast aside
. . . Who do not hide their sadness from . . . The least of company
. . . But make it obvious that they . . . Are starved for sympathy . . .
They feel so sorry for themselves . . . They wander everywhere . . .
In search of someone kind enough . . . To listen and to care . . .
While usually they are the ones . . . Who were not really spurned
. . . By some attractive soul for whom . . . Quite secretly they yearned
. . . They just assumed when someone said . . . "Good day, and
how are you?" . . . It meant, "I love you, marry me . . . I will be
always true."

COACH

He is the one who trains a team . . . With faith and expectation . . .
That someday it will be among . . . The best ones in the nation . . .
He drills and drives from day to day . . . To bring about perfection
. . . And boost morale, to give each boy . . . The healthiest complex-
ion . . . His time is taken up with things . . . Too numerous to men-
tion . . . Yet every player's problems get . . . His personal attention
. . . And as he strives to shape the skill . . . That wins in competition
. . . He hopes and prays that he will gain . . . His greatest recogni-
tion . . . Not by the scores and victories . . . Of physical collisions
. . . But building character in youth . . . To make the right decisions.

SO STRONG MY LOVE

Nothing on earth could take away . . . The love I have for you . . .
Not even anything my dear . . . That you might ever do . . . Not
even if you told me that . . . You cared for me no more . . . And if
you turned away and tried . . . To close and seal the door . . . Not
even if you laughed at me . . . And struck me on the face . . . Or
slandered me most viciously . . . In every public place . . . Yes, you
could really hurt my heart . . . And you could make me cry . . . And
cause me suffering until . . . I wished that I could die . . . And
bombs could blast the earth, the sky . . . And every ocean blue . . .
But nothing, darling, could destroy . . . The love I have for you.

PROTECT THEM, GOD

Dear God, protect our children now . . . As school vacation starts
. . . Grant them a happy summertime . . . And bless their eager
hearts . . . Watch over them in swimming pools . . . And on the
picnic ground . . . And everywhere on bicycles . . . They like to ride
around . . . Especially the ones in camp . . . Who are so far away . . .
That we cannot be with them through . . . The hours of the day . . .
Preserve them from grave illness and . . . From serious injury . . .
And by Your grace may there not be . . . A single tragedy . . . So
when the schoolbell rings, and when . . . The roll is called once more
. . . All of our children, safe and sound . . . Will be accounted for.

BETTER THAN GOLD

Friendship is a precious thing . . . More valuable than gold . . . A
treasure truly wonderful . . . For all to have and hold . . . It comforts
us in sorrow and . . . It gives us courage new . . . When everything
seems hopeless and . . . We know not what to do . . . It is our rainbow in the dawn . . . To end the wildest storm . . . The loving and
protecting arm . . . That keeps us safe and warm . . . Friendship is
the only way . . . That we can really share . . . Our joy in life that
otherwise . . . Would vanish into air . . . So let us treasure every
friend . . . Whom we may call our own . . . Without that blessing
on this earth . . . We would be all alone.

REUNIONS

No meetings can compare with those . . . Reunions that we hold
. . . To live again our memories . . . Those moments made of gold
. . . However young or old we are . . . We love those great conven-
tions . . . Where always some familiar name . . . Is one that someone
mentions . . . A banquet and a lunch or two . . . With faces everywhere . . . That happily remind us of . . . The time when we were
there . . . Reunions are the parties great . . . When good friends
get together . . . To talk about the olden days . . . Or just about the
weather . . . They are the bonds of kindred souls . . . That tie
around the heart . . . And seal the lasting promise that . . . Old
friends will never part.

LUCKY NUMBER

A lucky number is a thing . . . Some people find or choose . . . That
they regard a magic charm . . . By which they cannot lose . . . They
take it as a guiding star . . . In business or in play . . . To seek their
fortune in a game . . . Or on a certain day . . . It prompts them in
a baseball pool . . . Or when the ponies race . . . Or sets the time
for dealing with . . . The problems they must face . . . And if that
number fails them, they . . . Do not discard it then . . . But say it
was an accident . . . And try it out again . . . Until one day they
have to play . . . A number not their size . . . And oddly it turns out
to be . . . The one that wins the prize.

UNCLE SAM'S PAYDAY

Today is payday once again . . . But not for you or me . . . It is the
day our Uncle Sam . . . Receives his salary . . . It is the final hour
when . . . The income tax is due . . . The cash he needs for household bills . . . And others that accrue . . . With every cent that he
receives . . . Our commonweal increases . . . Because he spends it
all on us . . . His nephews and his nieces . . . Not just for current
needs and for . . . Old age security . . . But also to protect our
home . . . From every enemy . . . And so we should be glad to pay
. . . Each dollar and each dime . . . And see that Uncle Sam receives
. . . His salary on time.

SO PROUD AND HAPPY

There is no measurement on earth . . . However long or wide . . .
That could encircle or compute . . . My happiness and pride . . . The
pride and happiness, dear one . . . That you have given me . . . By
promising to be my own . . . For all eternity . . . There is no depth
by fathoms long . . . To match the way I feel . . . As now I promise
you my love . . . Forever warm and real . . . I promise you with all
my heart . . . To be forever true . . . And I will never go astray . . .
Or tell a lie to you . . . I will belong to you until . . . The final sun
has set . . . And you will never cry or have . . . One reason to regret.

PEACE WITHIN

When all around is noisy and . . . You cannot stand the din . . .
Seek not a silent hiding place . . . But pray for peace within . . . Do
not despair and run away . . . As you would like to do . . . Because
no matter where you turn . . . The noise will follow you . . . But if
you speak to God with hope . . . And sentiment sincere . . . It will
be just a while until . . . No sound will reach your ear . . . Except
the voice of God that brings . . . A calmness to your heart . . . To set
aside your smallest fear . . . And draw the world apart . . . If you
have faith in God and prayer . . . And promise not to sin . . . No
clamor can disturb the peace . . . That you will hold within.

DON'T BE FOOLISH

Today is April Fool's Day and . . . There are those many tricks . . .
Like pocketbooks with strings attached . . . And hats that cover bricks
. . . It is a special time for fun . . . And laughter loud and long . . .
But we should all be sensible . . . And not do any wrong . . . Some
jokes can be too practical . . . And carried quite too far . . . And
mighty dangerous can be . . . The net results there are . . . So let us
all be careful of . . . The tricks we play today . . . And cause no hurt
or injury . . . Along our jovial way . . . Let's fool each other and have
fun . . . But do it harmlessly . . . So this occasion will not turn . . .
Into a tragedy.

SOCIAL CIRCLE

Of all the circles in this life . . . The social kind is best . . . As it provides a medium . . . For thinking and for rest . . . The circle that is fashioned for . . . A group of ladies sweet . . . Who like to sew or knit and talk . . . Whenever they may meet . . . A group of men from college with . . . Their alma mater cheers . . . Now seriously pursuing their . . . Professional careers . . . Yes, even in the idle ranks . . . Of high society . . . The circle may produce some thought . . . And honest energy . . . The social circle is the best . . . If it surrounds the kind . . . Who seek not only to relax . . . But to improve the mind.

LIBRARY CARD

The public library gives out . . . A card that is a key . . . To anyone who would unlock . . . The door to history . . . The history of yesteryear . . . And all the years before . . . Of everything and each who made . . . A literary score . . . That little card is valuable . . . As its subscribers borrow . . . Whatever volumes they would keep . . . Until some set tomorrow . . . Sometimes forgetful patrons get . . . A little out of line . . . And having held their books too long . . . They have to pay a fine . . . But anyway you look at it . . . No pleasure could compare . . . With that small card that opens wide . . . The door to everywhere.

OLD ADDRESS BOOK

I have an old address book that . . . Is filled with names and places . . . And with a thousand memories . . . Of once familiar faces . . . The relatives or friends with whom . . . I used to correspond . . . Companions and acquaintances . . . Of whom I was so fond . . . Each yellow page is peppered with . . Deletions or revisions . . . As people moved and disappeared . . . Or God make the decisions . . . Once in a while I look through that . . . Address book on my shelf . . . And as I muse, I wonder what . . . Is happening to myself . . . Time changes everything, and yet . . . Each change is gradual . . . We scarcely notice it, because . . . It seems so casual.

PRAY FOR HOPE

Hope is our strongest tool in life . . . Stronger than faith itself . . .
Or any other implement . . . That may adorn our shelf . . . So dead-
end and so blind would be . . . The alley where we grope . . . Unless along the path of life . . . We always had some hope . . . It is a
gift from God to us . . . While we are on this earth . . . Our inspiration constantly . . . To be of better worth . . . Without it we would
walk with death . . . Despair, defeat and fear . . . And pass the sign,
"Abandon hope . . . All you who enter here" . . . So let us pray to
God that we . . . May keep our hope alive . . . And give His grace
to reach the goal . . . For which our souls would strive.

YOUR BOSS KNOWS

Perhaps you think that you could show . . . Your boss a thing or two
. . . If managing the office force . . . Was strictly up to you . . . And
possibly you even think . . . You have the business sense . . . To run
the firm, increase its gain . . . And lessen its expense . . . And
maybe you could do it too . . . But more than likely not . . . As you
have been unable to . . . Improve your present lot . . . Oh, yes, there
could be prejudice . . . Or jealousy or pride . . . With sneaky schemes
to interfere . . . And throw you off your stride . . . But if you were
so capable . . . You would not have to worry . . . Your boss would
recognize it and . . . Promote you in a hurry.

BE FRIENDLY

Every morning, noon and night . . . No matter what your mood . . .
Always do your best to show . . . A friendly attitude . . . Rain or
sunshine, snow or hail . . . Let others see your smile . . . Whatever
the occasion, it . . . Will well be worth your while . . . Try to hide
your hate as much . . . As you can cover it . . . Conceal your grudge,
and you will be . . . A noble hypocrite . . . The only time when it
becomes . . . A virtue to pretend . . . As you are eager to regain . . .
Or make another friend . . . And as you strive to be sincere . . . The
charity you do . . . Will be the bread the wind and waves . . . Will
soon return to you.

STEP AT A TIME

If you are lacking confidence . . . And walk in doubt and fear . . . Be not disturbed, as long as you . . . Are willing and sincere . . . For many famous persons were . . . Exceedingly afraid . . . Before they were convinced that they . . . Could really make the grade . . . And you will learn, the same as they . . . It is not overnight . . . But step by step along the way . . . To overcome your fright . . . With every step your faith will grow . . . If you will only try . . . And you will realize that it is . . . No use to quit or cry . . . Do everything you think you can . . . Then tackle something more . . . And as you build your confidence . . . So you will raise your score.

SILENT VOICE

A letter is the silent voice . . . Of paper and of ink . . . That tells the one to whom we write . . . The way we feel and think . . . A voice more calm and cautious than . . . The tongue inclines to be . . . Unless in anger, hate or such . . . The pen moves foolishly . . . A letter is the courier . . . Of tidings sad or good . . . Or just the news that all is well . . . Throughout the neighborhood . . . We use it for our business, and . . . To serve our social ends . . . By speaking in that manner to . . . Our relatives and friends . . . And then there is the letter that . . . Is kissed and put away . . . With other loving words that will . . . Be read again someday.

PRIVATE MAIL

The mail delivered to our home . . . Is private as can be . . . Addressed distinctly to my wife . . . The children or to me . . . I never open it unless . . . It obviously is mine . . . And I have always tried to keep . . . The family in line . . . I know I would not violate . . . The postal laws today . . . If I should open mail received . . . And read what it might say . . . No legal wrong would be involved . . . But quite a moral one . . . To peek at letters for my wife . . . Our daughter or our son . . . For family correspondence is . . . A very private thing . . . And there is never an excuse . . . For any tampering.

JUST WE

Do I need to tell you, dear . . . You are the only one? . . . Must I
thank you once again . . . For all that you have done? . . . Surely in
your heart you know . . . There is no doubt in mine . . . If you gazed
into my eyes . . . You must have seen the sign . . . Every hope I
have in life . . . All I want to do . . . Is just to help you and to bring
. . . More happiness to you . . . all I ask you in return . . . Is just
your love for me . . . Golden hours that become . . . A timeless memory . . . Not security or wealth . . . Or any earthly fame . . . But just
the bondage of our hearts . . . In our united name.

PRAY FOR WEALTH?

It is not wrong to pray to God . . . For worldly happiness . . . Or
even any measure of . . . Material success . . . Unless in our ambition for . . . A throne beneath the sun . . . Our underlying motive is . . . A purely selfish one . . . If we are thinking only of . . .
The joy that we would know . . . And not about the good on
earth . . . Our fortune could bestow . . . Then surely we do not
deserve . . . To have our dreams come true . . . And likely they
will fade, as God . . . Knows all we plan to do . . . But if we mean
our fortune to . . . Be well and wisely spent . . . God will consider our request . . . And help to that extent.

I'LL GET IT!

Each time the phone or doorbell rings . . . I feel we ought to let
it . . . But always there is somebody . . . Who hollers out, "I'll get
it!" . . . It's usually the children who . . . Are dashing to the door
. . . Or snatching up the phone to hear . . . Some voice they're
waiting for . . . Though sometimes it is Mommy who . . . Will
get there in a hurry . . . With great excitement in her eyes . . .
Or with a look of worry . . . I never get there first but if . . . The
call should be for me . . . I see those disappointed looks . . .
Throughout the family . . . I hesitate to answer rings . . . I fear
I may regret it . . . But not my wife or youngsters who . . . Will
always yell, "I'll get it!"

A FAVOR IS A GIFT

No favor we receive becomes . . . An obligation true . . . To carry out the smallest task . . . We may be asked to do . . . Because a favor is a gift . . . And not a bargain made . . . Whereby our deeds of charity . . . Are merely things we trade . . . If any help is based upon . . . A promise to repay . . . Then it is just a business deal . . . And not a "give-away" . . . It may be very timely and . . . Involve a great expense . . . But it is not a favor in . . . The very slightest sense . . . A favor is a present with . . . No string attached to it . . . And never any invoice that . . . Demands that we remit.

WILD WEST TODAY

If there is something in the West . . . That still is really wild . . . It surely is not something I . . . Remember as a child . . . It is no holster and a gun . . . A quick and ready draw . . . An Indian or buffalo . . . Or badman that I saw . . . For there is really nothing wild . . . About the Western way . . . Except as people disregard . . . Our traffic laws today . . . They are the wildest humans when . . . Their hands are on the wheel . . . And they don't care the least about . . . How other people feel . . . They are the wildest and the worst . . . Just out for late-night fun . . . Until they run down and they kill . . . Some loving mother's son.

HOW LEARNED YOU?

What has your schooling done for you? . . . How has your thinking grown? . . . Do you stand out above the crowd . . . With knowledge all your own? . . . Do you believe your high school or . . . Your university . . . Has mentally endowed you with . . . Superiority? . . . Then you have failed to make the grade . . . Your learning has been lost . . . And those long years you spent in school . . . Have not been worth the cost . . . Because the more you learn, the more . . . Your humbleness should grow . . . As now you realize there is still . . . So much you do not know . . . Your education should be such . . . That you need envy none . . . And such that you will not disdain . . . The less instructed one.

LET ME REPEAT

If now I say some words to you . . . That you have heard before
. . . I want to tell you, darling, that . . . I mean them more and
more . . . However often I repeat . . . The smallest phrase of love
. . . Remember it is only you . . . Whom I am thinking of . . .
Remember that your happiness . . . Is my important goal . . . And
repetition, darling, is . . . So good for every soul . . . And so I
say those words again . . . As often as I may . . . With every whisper from my heart . . . Throughout each night and day . . . With
every letter that I send . . . And on the telephone . . . As we are
separated or . . . Together all alone.

PRAYER FOR PRUDENCE

Help me, O God, to live a life . . . Of prudence every day . . .
In exercising judgment and . . . In all I do and say . . . Let not my
thoughts be hurried now . . . Let not my passions rule . . . Nor let
my tongue in idleness . . . Reveal me as a fool . . . But give me grace
and guidance to . . . Avoid the least excess . . . In my pursuit of any
form . . . Of earthly happiness . . . For I would rather end my days
. . . In humbleness, alone . . . Than reach the smallest sinful height
. . . For which I must atone . . . Help me, O God, to practice now
. . . The prudence that I need . . . To honor You and serve You
well . . . In thought and word and deed.

WRITER'S LIFE

I figure out the days ahead . . . As ably as I can . . . But seldom is it possible . . . To carry out my plan . . . If I decide to write
all night . . . Then sleep late in the day . . . I feel a sudden rest-
lessness . . . That makes my thinking stray . . . And if instead I
go to bed . . . And greet the early dawn . . . I join the family
breakfast and . . . My will to work is gone . . . The choice is mine
to spend my time . . . However I may choose . . . But just as defi-
nitely is . . . My chance to win or lose . . . How fortunate are
those who have . . . A boss from day to day . . . To tell them what
and when to do . . . And guide them on their way!

TO START ANEW

If there is any hope in life . . . It is the knowledge true . . . That
as almighty God forgives . . . So we may start anew . . . However
dark our past may be . . . However filled with sin . . . There still
is opportunity . . . To struggle and to win . . . But we must have
the courage and . . . The faith and vision clear . . . And, more
important than all else . . . We have to be sincere . . . And we
must do the best we can . . . In every way to bring . . . A compensation to each one . . . We caused some suffering . . . And yet
how little this becomes . . . For anyone to do . . . Considering
the blessing of . . . The chance to start anew!

ALLEY

An alley is not just a place . . . Where garbage cans must wait
. . . Until collectors come around . . . To keep their certain date
. . . It is a short-cut to the store . . . Or to a football field . . . Or
it may be a No-Man's Land . . . Where neighbors never yield . . .
It is a place where youngsters play . . . With marbles in a ring . . .
Or groups in search of charity . . . Strike up their band and sing
. . . An alley is the boulevard . . . For those who spend their lives
. . . In search of rags, old iron and . . . The chance to sharpen
knives . . . It is the path that lies between . . . The back-yards of
our nation . . . Where everyone is equal in . . . The scheme of
God's creation.

WONDERFUL MAY

May is the month of flowers fair . . . With gorgeous skies above
. . . Deep in the springtime of the year . . . The season made for
love . . . May is the month for city parks . . . And playgrounds
everywhere . . . When children ride their bikes, while they . . . Ignore their tousled hair . . . The time to wrap up final plans . . .
For summertime vacations . . . Away from home and office and
. . . Perhaps from some relations . . . Yes, May is really wonderful
. . . With hopes so bright and new . . . And with the wondrous
wishes that . . . We wish would all come true . . . It is indeed a
merry month . . . As many people say . . . And every year, by God's
good grace . . . May it go on that way.

GARDEN OF DREAMS

Tonight I met you at a dance . . . And yet, my dear, it seems . . .
I first beheld your beauty in . . . The garden of my dreams . . .
And that was many years ago . . . When I was just a child . . . And
I was so in love with all . . . The flowers that grew wild . . . I
whispered all my secrets in . . . A very special place . . . And that
is where one day I saw . . . Your sweet, enchanting face . . . And
now I know that you are real . . . I hold you in my arms . . . And,
darling, I am overwhelmed . . . By all your many charms . . . Dear
one, you are the only one . . . In all my thoughts and schemes
. . . You are the fairest flower in . . . The garden of my dreams.

NO SECRET FROM GOD

You may have many secrets that . . . Are sensible or odd . . .
But there is not a single one . . . That you can keep from God
. . . Because He hears your every word . . . He sees all things you
do . . . And in the last analysis . . . He knows your thinking too
. . . Yes, you may hide from all the world . . . And feel that you
are free . . . Quite sure your special secret is . . . Beyond discovery
. . . But God, who made the earth and you . . . Knows all your
hopes and dreams . . . Your daily virtues and your faults . . . And
your most secret schemes . . . However brilliant you may be . . .
Whatever time or tide . . . From God, your Lord and Master there
. . . Is nothing you can hide.

SMART PRETZEL

Our dachshund, Pretzel, never went . . . To any kind of school
. . . Yet he is not a stupid dog . . . By any law or rule . . . For he
is smart enough to know . . . When it is time to eat . . . To find
his way outside the house . . . Or slumber at our feet . . . He
yawns each time we ask him to . . . And he sits up for us . . . Prepared to kiss us sloppily . . . With all his canine fuss . . . He is a
watchdog wonderful . . . That barks at every sound . . . To let us
know that possibly . . . Some strangers are around . . . Yes, he is
smart but there is still . . . Another explanation . . . We love him,
and he wants to show . . . His deep appreciation.

WHY WORRY?

Each day the headlines look more black . . . As tragedies occur . . .
And yet they are not really worse . . . Than those that always were
. . . When we compare statistics on . . . The dangers long ago
. . . Remember population and . . . How fast today we grow . . .
Of course there are those accidents . . . And crimes that some commit . . . That make it seem today there are . . . So many more
unfit . . . But things are not so different from . . . The days that
now are gone . . . As we have always found a way . . . To live and
carry on . . . Somehow we meet each obstacle . . . And overcome
the odds . . . As we believe and finally . . . Our destiny is God's.

SMALL TOWN TODAY

The small town used to be the one . . . Where everybody knew
. . . Your family, your history . . . And all you tried to do . . .
And there are still those towns that judge . . . Your life from day
to day . . . With gossip based on guesses when . . . You chance to
go away . . . But now there are those little towns . . . Outside the
cities tall . . . Where scarcely any residents . . . Are working there
at all . . . Where most of them commute by bus . . . Suburban
train or car . . . And seldom take the time to learn . . . Just who
their neighbors are . . . Commuters quite contented as . . . In privacy they live . . . Who never know the warmth and love . . . A
real small town can give.

OUR TEARS AND THANKS

The bugle leaves a soldier's lips . . . The echo fades away . . . All
heads are bowed in silence as . . . We meditate and pray . . . The
Stars and Stripes are lowered now . . . By hands that reverently
. . . Salute our sons who fought and died . . . For peace and liberty . . . We contemplate the courage true . . . Of those who gave
their all . . . As we ask God to cover them . . . With His protective
shawl . . . And we give thanks to everyone . . . Who wore a uniform . . . And served our country faithfully . . . In time of stress
and storm . . . All veterans of every war . . . Who did their best
to strive . . . For justice and equality . . . To keep the world alive.

CONFIDENCE

Confidence is not a thing . . . That simply comes our way . . . It has to be developed as . . . We grow from day to day . . . It must come from experience . . . In things we have to do . . . Supported by our interest in . . . The course that we pursue . . . And most of all our willingness . . . To struggle hard and long . . . Until our hearts achieve that goal . . . Of faith and courage strong . . . And it is worth the effort and . . . The time to cultivate . . . If we would render services . . . That could be truly great . . . Services to God and home . . . And all the neighborhood . . . As we are confident that we . . . Can really do some good.

TEACH EVERY CHILD

There is no greater blessing for . . . A child upon this sod . . . Than just to learn the story true . . . Of our almighty God . . . To know that he or she is here . . . Because God granted life . . . And He will help each soul to meet . . . The struggle and the strife . . . And there is no one worse on earth . . . Than someone who denies . . . The truth as it is known to us . . . And tells the children lies . . . It may be out of ignorance . . . Of hatred or of fear . . . But it is cruel and unjust . . . To all our children dear . . . Each boy and girl belongs to God . . . And each should know its worth . . . That only by the grace of God . . . Is he or she on earth.

DECEMBER 26TH

The morning after Christmas is . . . A morning to remember . . . The dawning of the 26th . . . With headaches in December . . . With headaches for the housewife and . . . The mother tired out . . . Who finds that wrappings, cards and toys . . . Are scattered all about . . . And there are stores that ladies storm . . . To make a quick exchange . . . Sometimes insisting on a price . . . Within a higher range . . . It is a day of headaches great . . . For business and for wives . . . Which seemingly does not affect . . . The husbands' daily lives . . . Except as they eventually . . . Will have to pay each debit . . . And to repair each broken toy . . . Without the smallest credit.

YOUR STARLIT EYES

I used to think the twinkling stars . . . Were only in the skies . . .
But now I know that two of them . . . Are those that light your
eyes . . . Two starlit eyes so beautiful . . . So wonderfully entrancing . . . With music drifting softly while . . . Your dainty feet are
dancing . . . In your enchanting gaze, my love . . . The whole
world fades away . . . There are no more tomorrows and . . . There
is no yesterday . . . This magic moment is our own . . . And it
will leave us never . . . This happiness is ours to hold . . . Forever
and forever . . . Two star-kissed eyes, two star-filled eyes . . . Like
angels from above . . . Embracing me and blessing me . . . With
everlasting love.

FAMOUS DEEDS

Our famous deeds appear to be . . . The only ones that last . . .
The rest, no matter what their worth . . . Are buried in the past
. . . Our deeds must be outstanding, and . . . Get wide publicity
. . . To gain enduring character . . . In public memory . . . They
need not have much virtue, nor . . . Be truly glorious . . . Indeed
some have no moral worth . . . They are notorious . . . But why
should public memory . . . Mean anything at all . . . Except as
deeds are virtuous . . . Examples to recall? . . . Our good acts are
remembered by . . . The ones who benefit . . . And God knows
every deed, and keeps . . . A true account of it.

FLOWER VENDOR

He sells his flowers on the street . . . To people passing by . . . He
does not ask their purpose but . . . He knows each reason why
. . . He recognizes bashful beaus . . . In search of bright bouquets
. . . And lady shoppers who just want . . . Some lovely little sprays
. . . The faithful husband, homeward bound . . . Who cherishes
his wife . . . The gay old business blade who thinks . . . He still
has lots of life . . . Carnation, rose and violet . . . And every other
bloom . . . With fragrance that surrounds the heart . . . And dissipates all gloom . . . He does not probe the problems of . . . The
people he may meet . . . He simply peddles beauty that . . . Will
help the world smell sweet.

ANOTHER WEEK

The church bells now are ringing out . . . The doors are open wide
. . . And God Himself is beckoning . . . To have you come inside
. . . It is His house of worship and . . . Your place to kneel and
pray . . . Especially on Sunday morn . . . But also every day . . . His
heart is always waiting there . . . To listen to your tears . . . To put
away your troubles and . . . To calm your smallest fears . . . So go to
church on Sunday and . . . Be honest with your God . . . As much
as He allows you now . . . To live upon this sod . . . Be grateful for
His help in all . . . The glory that you seek . . . And ask Him to protect your soul . . . For just another week.

NO END TO LEARNING

In high school and in college we . . . Look forward to the day
. . . When we can close our study books . . . And put them all
away . . . We think that school is limited . . . And when that time
is through . . . The world is ours in which to thrive . . . As we may
wish to do . . . Yes, schooldays will be over but . . . Our learning
never ends . . . As we pursue this puzzling life . . . With enemies
and friends . . . We have to keep on studying . . . The world and
all its ways . . . And even in our dotage we . . . May still be in a
daze . . . So let us learn each lesson for . . . Whatever it is worth
. . . And take our time in our attempt . . . To conquer all the earth.

KRISTINA DREAMS

Kristina had a dream last night . . . And maybe it was queer . . .
But in her morning memory . . . I know that it was clear . . . And
I am grateful for her thoughts . . . However strange or mild . . .
Because she said she never dreamed . . . When she was just a
child . . . I always used to wonder if . . . She slept just like a rock
. . . Or if she saw some vision she . . . Kept under key and lock
. . . So now Kristina seems to be . . . A normal girl at last . . .
With pictures in her slumber of . . . The present and the past . . .
I only hope her future dreams . . . Will all be good and glad . . .
And she will have no nightmare that . . . Involves her loving dad.

YOU ARE MY SPRING

Spring is here again, my love . . . That wondrous time of year . . . When nature gives the whole wide world . . . A new-born atmosphere . . . Spring reminds me of the days . . . When first we came together . . . And walked and talked, while holding hands . . . Unmindful of the weather . . . There is a certain something in . . . This season of the year . . . That makes us smile, and keeps away . . . The very smallest tear . . . Of course, I love you every day . . . Regardless of the season . . . And anyone who knows you, dear . . . Would recognize the reason . . . But you are so enchanting that . . . Together or apart . . . I cannot help but feel that spring . . . Is always in my heart.

PROJECT

A project is a task we plan . . . With thoughtfulness and care . . . Not just a sudden notion or . . . A castle in the air . . . It is a resolution to . . . Perform a certain thing . . . With avid concentration on . . . Results that it can bring . . . The main ingredient it needs . . . Is perseverance true . . . No project is of consequence . . . Unless we see it through . . . Also, no project can deserve . . . The smallest word of praise . . . Unless it does some good on earth . . . In one of worthy ways . . . A project is a promise which . . . When once we have begun . . . Is meaningless unless we do . . . Our best to get it done.

EQUALLY FRIENDS

It matters not how long ago . . . I saw a friend of mine . . . Or who picked up the dinner check . . . When we went out to dine . . . As long as he comes back to me . . . And shares my humble table . . . With food and drink of every kind . . . As much as I am able . . . As long as he remembers me . . . And wants to be my friend . . . Until tomorrow morning and . . . Forever without end . . . There can be interruptions in . . . A friendship of long standing . . . But there are always bridges when . . . No one is too demanding . . . There is no friendship in this world . . . That ever will be lost . . . If we are truly faithful and . . . Prepared to share the cost.

WAITING

Waiting is so lonely and . . . So very anxious too , . . . Waiting just
for someone, or . . . To have a dream come true . . . Waiting for
tomorrow, or . . . Some other special day . . . When something
very wonderful . . . Is due to come your way . . . Waiting with a
fearful heart . . . When slim recovery . . . Is all the chance a doctor has . . . Against a tragedy . . . Waiting while you hope somehow . . . It turns out for the best . . . Always waiting, day and
night . . . With little sleep or rest . . . Waiting for a phone call or
. . . Arrival of a train . . . Nothing else can do so much . . . To
tax the human brain.

ANOTHER START

Whatever prayer I say tonight . . . It could not make amends . . .
For all the injuries that I . . . Have done to all my friends . . .
And yet I ask forgiveness for . . . My failures of today . . . And
beg You, God, for one more chance . . . To live a better way . . .
As much as I am human and . . . My body has to live . . . I ask
You now sincerely to . . . Forget and to forgive . . . Give me the
opportunity . . . To make another start . . . And help me be con-
siderate . . . And gentle in my heart . . . I want to be Your servant,
God . . . In everything I do . . . So when I die my soul will be . . .
Acceptable to You.

LOCAL LEVEL

If we could help make certain that . . . Our country shall not fail
. . . We should extend our efforts on . . . The local, civic scale . . .
Because the hometown level is . . . The powerful foundation . . .
On which, with methods tried and true . . . Is built our mighty
nation . . . It is that local unity . . . Of shoulders to the wheel . . .
That binds our brotherhood, and makes . . . Democracy so real . . .
Let us display our willingness . . . As now we get together . . . To
serve our own community . . . In every kind of weather . . . How-
ever large our city or . . . How small our hamlet's size . . . Let us
promote with heart and soul . . . Each civic enterprise.

I DREAMED OF YOU

I dreamed of you last night, my love . . . I dreamed that you were mine . . . And in your happy eyes I saw . . . The stars and moonbeams shine . . . We had a little house with trees . . . And flowers all around . . . And there we two had all the joy . . . And peace that could be found . . . The birds were singing merrily . . . The sky was bright and clear . . . And in a cradle at our side . . . We rocked our baby dear . . . We stood there holding hands, and then . . . We shared the sweetest kiss . . . And felt that nothing else could be . . . As wonderful as this . . . I only wish it had not been . . . Just one more dream of you . . . But, oh, I hope and pray some day . . . That vision will come true!

LETTER OPENER

The letter opener is a key . . . To friendship, love and bills . . . To gossip and more truthful news . . . Of people's joys and ills . . . It slices envelopes to bring . . . Their contents into sight . . . Exciting, somewhat frightening . . . Or calm and quite all right . . . A summons to appear in court . . . A party invitation . . . A check to pay, a pension or . . . Some other compensation . . . The letter opener is one . . . We purchase at a store . . . Or in a gift-wrapped package is . . . Delivered to our door . . . It is a business instrument . . . Or else a souvenir . . . Engraved with thanks for service or . . . By someone very dear.

WONDERFUL HOME

No place is more appealing than . . . The home you call your own . . . Unless you have no family . . . And you must live alone . . . Your visit to a mansion or . . . A palace bright and gay . . . May make you quite delirious . . . And take your breath away . . . Your dearest friends may ask you in . . . To visit for a while . . . And there may be a cozy hearth . . . And everywhere a smile . . . However far, however long . . . Your search for joy goes on . . . There is no warmer happiness . . . Than being home at dawn . . . And you may sail the seven seas . . . And other places roam . . . But nowhere will you find a place . . . As wonderful as home.

WEEP NOT TOO MUCH

It is all right to feel regret . . . But not a deep remorse . . . Your condemnation of yourself . . . Can throw you off your course . . . Do be contrite and shed a tear . . . But never take the view . . . That you have been so sinful that . . . There is no hope for you . . . Do not surrender to despair . . . Let not your courage break . . . Keep on contributing your best . . . For someone else's sake . . . God wants you to have faith in Him . . . And not succumb to fear . . . And He will always love you if . . . You strive to be sincere . . . So do not let your mind build up . . . A self-reproaching story . . . God understands, and He forgives . . . When you are really sorry.

APRIL RAIN

Rain is pouring down today . . . But it is bringing cheer . . . Because it is so welcome, now . . . That April days are here . . . Rain belongs to April and . . . The seeds we plant with care . . . Especially to help design . . . May's gown of flowers fair . . . April showers melt the snow . . . On highway and on street . . . And lift umbrellas under which . . . Sometimes young lovers meet . . . April rain is helpful to . . . The farmer and his crops . . . Though now and then there may be just . . . A few too many drops . . . It washes cobwebs from our minds . . . To make our vision clear . . . So we can see and we can feel . . . That spring once more is here.

KRISSIE MAY DRIVE

Krissie, sweet sixteen, has passed . . . The test to drive a car . . . So now she is allowed by law . . . To motor near and far . . . I cannot quite describe the pride . . . And happiness I feel . . . In knowing that our daughter can . . . Manipulate that wheel . . . And I am not afraid for her . . . Because she seems to be . . . Just like her mommy dear who drives . . . So well and cautiously . . . I know our Krissie will obey . . . Each traffic rule and sign . . . So she will cause no accident . . . Or draw the smallest fine . . . Just one thing does disturb me now . . . As she appears so grown . . . She may be asking for a car . . . To be her very own.

LOVING TREASURE

I treasure your embraces and . . . Your kisses so sincere . . . Each letter that you write becomes . . . A precious souvenir . . . I want you always, dearest one . . . Sweet angel at my side . . . For faith and hope and courage and . . . My pardonable pride . . . My pride that you have promised me . . . Your love for evermore . . . And all the wondrous joys . . . That life may hold in store . . . I treasure you and always will . . . Wherever you may go . . . Because you are so charming and . . . Because I love you so . . . I want to keep you deep inside . . . My safe deposit box . . . Where no one else can get the keys . . . To open both the locks.

OUR ALL TO GOD

Unless we give ourselves to God . . . In everything we do . . . We cannot hope for help from Him . . . To see our problems through . . . There is no half-way deal with Him . . . With so much time to pray . . . And all the rest in which to go . . . Our own, unthinking way . . . But we must serve Him always with . . . Our love and kindly care . . . As we bestow them gladly on . . . His creatures everywhere . . . There is no compromise between . . . Humility and pride . . . Nor any sin, however slight . . . That we can ever hide . . . We have to give ourselves to God . . . With all our heart and soul . . . If ever we have hope to reach . . . The glory of our goal.

WE MUST DECIDE

Friends who give advice mean well . . . And sometimes what they say . . . Is logical and helpful in . . . A most substantial way . . . But no advice, however good . . . Can be per se the best . . . For what may cure a few may not . . . Be tonic for the rest . . . Indeed the very opposite . . . Could be the medicine . . . Which some require to go on . . . And give their all to win . . . There is no harm in listening to . . . Advice from every side . . . But only the recipient . . . Should finally decide . . . God blest us with a mind and with . . . The freedom of our will . . . As humanly as possible . . . Our future to fulfill.

BLIND HYPOCRITES

No man can be a hypocrite . . . When he is all alone . . . For how
can he deceive himself . . . With words that are his own? . . . This
was the teaching long ago . . . Of thoughts and actions done . . .
As once it was expounded by . . . Ralph Waldo Emerson . . . And
there is truth in that today . . . But it does not apply . . . To hypo-
crites who go so far . . . They do not know they lie . . . Some hypo-
crites pursue their course . . . Of what they strive to do . . . Until
their minds become convinced . . . Their thoughts are really true
. . . They follow their ambitious way . . . Until the day they
die . . . With no concern their every word . . . May be another lie.

CAN

A can is a container for . . . The stuff we eat and drink . . . But
it is not a mere "tin can" . . . As some of us may think . . . Today
the can is made of steel . . . With hardly any tin . . . And wonderfully are preserved . . . The products put therein . . . It seems to
be a simple thing . . . Upon the grocery shelves . . . That saves us
time and work when we . . . Are cooking for ourselves . . . But
seldom do we realize all . . . The research and the brains . . .
That help to hold the vitamins . . . A little can contains . . . It is
another miracle . . . Of science on its way . . . To bring the world
a better and . . . A healthier today.

WHEN THEY COME HOME

The day and night are lonely when . . . Our loved ones are away
. . . And even though the skies are clear . . . The atmosphere is
gray . . . There is a stillness in the house . . . That seems to split
the ear . . . Or is the ticking of the clock . . . That pounding noise
we hear? . . . But happy is that moment when . . . The mailman
rings the bell . . . And receive a message that . . . Our loved ones all
are well . . . And joyous is the hour when . . . The door is opened
wide . . . For sparkling eyes and laughing lips . . . To bring their
warmth inside . . . Not all the gold in all the world . . . Could
ever take the place . . . Or match the gay emotion of . . . That family
embrace.

GOD AT MY SIDE

Never in all my days on earth . . . Has God deserted me . . . He has
been always at my side . . . With soothing sympathy . . . He has forgiven me my sins . . . Each time I was contrite . . . Blest me each
dawn with breath to live . . . And rested me at night . . . God has
been bountiful to me . . . In all the ways there are . . . With inspiration from the sun . . . The moon and every star . . . He has not
favored me above . . . Anyone else on earth . . . He does the same
for every soul . . . That by His grace has birth . . . This should be
obvious to all . . . And never strange or odd . . . A fact that is self-
evident . . . If we believe in God.

RAINDROPS

Some raindrops fall upon the ground . . . Some kiss a windowpane
. . . All are the small components of . . . The blessing that is rain
. . . A rain can be quite treacherous . . . When it becomes too
much . . . Creating floods or joining hands . . . With hurricanes
and such . . . But little raindrops by themselves . . . Are not a
cruel lot . . . They are the sprinklers for a lawn . . . Or for a garden
plot . . . And more importantly they quench . . . The thirst of corn
and wheat . . . And make thermometers reflect . . . A little less of
heat . . . Raindrops are the angel-tears . . . That trickle from above
. . . Tears of joy for humans blessed . . . With God's enduring love.

FATHERLY ADVICE

A father tries to give advice . . . As Children start to grow . . . The
kind of wisdom his own dad . . . Imparted years ago . . . But somehow as he talks to them . . . It does not sound the same . . . And
silently he tells himself . . . His efforts are quite lame . . . He wants
to teach his youngsters, and . . . To guide them sensibly . . . But
feels that he can never match . . . His dad's philosophy . . . And
then one day his grown-up son . . . Or daughter with a beau . . .
Give thanks to him for some advice . . . Imparted long ago . . .
And suddenly it dawns on him . . . And sinks into his head . . .
He must have done a little good . . . With something he once said.

WHY I AM HAPPY

Why do I look so happy now? . . . Why is my heart so gay? . . . It
is because you love me, and . . . You make me feel that way . . .
Just being near you is enough . . . To please and comfort me . . .
But hearing you declare your love . . . Is truly ecstasy . . . It is
the magic wand that makes . . . My sweetest dream come true . . .
And promises a paradise . . . Of happiness with you . . . I thank
you for the sacred vow . . . You say that you will take . . . And
in return my life will be . . . For your beloved sake . . . There is
no other cause for joy . . . As life and love allow . . . This is the
only reason why . . . I am so happy now.

EARN AS YOU GO

The fairest pay for any work . . . That there could ever be . . . Is
that of a commission or . . . A certain royalty . . . A guaranteed
percentage of . . . The profit that is made . . . According to your
salesmanship . . . And how you make the grade . . . Because your
rate of pay is such . . . That you can only win . . . As your en-
deavors do their part . . . To bring the business in . . . Your peri-
odic check may be . . . Of large or little size . . . But it is what you
really earned . . . And therefore no surprise . . . Some salaries
appear too high . . . Some wages look too low . . . But when you
work percentage-wise . . . You earn it as you go.

MILITARY SCHOOL

The military high school is . . . A boon for many boys . . . With
discipline and study and . . . With gentlemanly joys . . . It teaches
truth and loyalty . . . Along their youthful way . . . And the signif-
icance of rules . . . That they must all obey . . . They are the
future students of . . . Our great academies . . . Where generals
and admirals . . . Preserve their memories . . . Of course there are
those certain boys . . . Who constantly insist . . . They do not want
commissions and . . . They care not to enlist . . . But military high
schools are . . . Of wondrous inspiration . . . As they inspire grad-
uates . . . To help protect our nation.

WHEN WE ARE WRONG

However brilliant we may be . . . However big and strong . . . It takes a lot of courage to . . . Admit that we are wrong . . . To actually acknowledge that . . . Somebody else knows more . . . And take our lesser place in line . . . Instead of getting sore . . . Sometimes we get real angry and . . . Insist that we are right . . . And just to prove a certain point . . . We are prepared to fight . . . Though there has never been a bout . . . Inside the mental ring . . . Where any kind of fisticuffs . . . Has settled anything . . . Why not admit that we are wrong . . . And take that battlescar? . . . And show by our admission now . . . How really big we are?

RAILROAD

The railroad is a carrier . . . Of people and of freight . . . To haul that special merchandise . . . Or keep a business date . . . It is the magic carpet that . . . Is guided by the rails . . . According to a schedule strict . . . That almost never fails . . . And there are letters on those trains . . . With worry, love or patience . . . That are protected carefully . . . To reach their destinations . . . The railroad serves our country well . . . In time of peace and war . . . And in so many happy ways . . . It gives a little more . . . The summer rates for tourists and . . . That added luxury . . . For those who need not be concerned . . . About economy.

DECEMBER IS HERE

December is a distant month . . . But it is here today . . . As autumn turns to winter and . . . The leaves are blown away . . . In August and July it seemed . . . This month would never be . . . As summer turned the lock on life . . . And kept the only key . . . But here it is December and . . . The snow is on the ground . . . And icy is the atmosphere . . . That settles all around . . . And yet there is no cause to be . . . Concerned with any strife . . . December joins the calendar . . . As long as there is life . . . And each December promises . . . As much of love and joy . . . As anybody could expect . . . For every girl and boy.

LOVE HAS TO GROW

You wonder if I love you, and . . . You ask some proof right now
. . . Before your heart agrees with mine . . . To share that sacred
vow . . . Well, that is quite impossible . . . For anyone to do . . .
You must believe me, darling, that . . . I am in love with you . . .
You have to judge me for yourself . . . With every thought and
glance . . . And in the last analysis . . . You have to take a chance
. . . Because there is no proof of love . . . Until the years go by
. . . And there is constant evidence . . . In every song and sigh
. . . Love is no sudden sentiment . . . That will forever glow . . .
It is a mutual feeling, dear . . . That has to grow and grow.

HOW MUCH FOR GOD?

God gave you your abilities . . . But it is up to you . . . To ask
His grace to guide you in . . . The tasks you have to do . . . However talented you are . . . You cannot win your way . . . Unless
you humbly ask your God . . . For help from day to day . . . You
may ignore Him and you may . . . Still find some happiness . . .
And you may reach the height of what . . . You think is real success . . . But what if you acquire all . . . The glory on this earth?
. . . What would you do with it, and what . . . Would be your final
worth? . . . Remember, you must face your God . . . For all eternity
. . . And He will ask, "In all your life . . . What did you do for Me?"

INVENTOR

He truly is a genius of . . . The most important kind . . . Who thinks
of new inventions with . . . An ever fertile mind . . . The young
inventor or the old . . . Whatever be his age . . . Who adds to progress in this world . . . Another helpful page . . . He is the source of
comforts that . . . Increase from day to day . . . And how to grow in
knowledge in . . . A faster, easier way . . . Sometimes his genius may
produce . . . A thing of doubtful worth . . . As it might help humanity . . . Or could destroy the earth . . . Yet he is indispensable . . .
To help fulfill our dreams . . . Unless the only thoughts he has . . .
Are cruel, fiendish schemes.

CAVEAT EMPTOR

In law there is a term that says . . . "Let him who buys beware" . . .
And maybe it is reasonable . . . And maybe it is fair . . . But if I
were the seller of . . . Some fake commodity . . . I know my conscience would revolt . . . And it would frighten me . . . And even if
the article . . . Were genuine in part . . . Unless the price were truly
right . . . It would disturb my heart . . . I would not wear a legal
cloak . . . To cheat and to deceive . . . The ones who heard or read
my word . . . That caused them to believe . . . In my philosophy
each price . . . Would have to be most fair . . . And not the pur-
chaser but I . . . Would ever need beware.

EVENING NAP

Evening is that special time . . . Not ever soon or late . . . It is the
bridge from day to night . . . On which to meditate . . . It is the
passageway that leads . . . From daily work to rest . . . With peace
and comfort and perhaps . . . The pleasure of a guest . . . That quiet
hour of reprieve . . . From every business care . . . When you embrace your family . . . And favorite easy chair . . . When weariness is
oozing out . . . Of every pore and vein . . . And as you start to nap,
each loss . . . Becomes another gain . . . And just before you fall
asleep . . . You see your sweetheart smile . . . And tell yourself the
evening nap . . . Makes everything worth while.

CURE FOR A COLD

I wish I had a penny now . . . For every remedy . . . My many friends
are offering . . . To cure the cold in me . . . I could possess a lim-
ousine . . . And walk on Persian rugs . . . Except, of course, for all
the cash . . . I'd have to spend on drugs . . . And all the money that
would go . . . For lemonade and milk . . . And formulas all guaranteed . . . To work as smooth as silk . . . My friends are most so-
licitous . . . And I appreciate . . . Their efforts to restore my health
. . . At some near future date . . . But after countless recipes . . .
My cold remains today . . . And so I think that I'll just wait . . . Until it goes away.